ASST Novels

WHEN THE FORESTS ARE ABLAZE

More useful so than a charred stub after a fire
[Page 62]

WHEN THE FORESTS ARE ABLAZE

BY

KATHARINE B. JUDSON

AUTHOR OF "MYTHS AND LEGENDS OF CALIFORNIA AND THE
OLD SOUTHWEST," "MYTHS AND LEGENDS OF ALASKA,"
"MYTHS AND LEGENDS OF THE PACIFIC
NORTHWEST," AND "MONTANA"

ILLUSTRATED
FROM PHOTOGRAPHS

CHICAGO
A. C. McCLURG & CO.
1912

PRESS OF THE VAIL COMPANY
COSHOCTON, U. S. A.

DEDICATED

TO

"THE MOUNTAINEERS"

WHOSE OBJECT IT IS TO PRESERVE THE MARVELOUS BEAUTY
OF THE PACIFIC NORTHWEST
AND WHO ARE YEARLY APPALLED BY THE
HAVOC OF THE FOREST FIRES

CONTENTS

CHAPTER   PAGE

I	THE PARODY	11
II	WHERE THE STORM WINDS BLOW	30
III	BEGINNINGS	50
IV	ON THE TRAIL	65
V	BURNHAM'S CABIN	87
VI	GETTING SETTLED	99
VII	THE BERRY PATCH	111
VIII	DOUGHNUTS	130
IX	THE DOUGLAS FIR	146
X	IMPROVEMENTS	160
XI	"BROOKSIDE"	176
XII	HUNTING	182
XIII	MY CABIN	208
XIV	CHRISTMAS	221
XV	THE TERROR OF THE FOREST	245
XVI	THE SQUATTER	264
XVII	UP THE VALLEY	277
XVIII	ON THE PEAK	299
XIX	HOPE DENHAM AGAIN	315
XX	DANGER	323
XXI	WHEN THE FORESTS BURN	333
XXII	FIRE AND WATER	346
XXIII	ILLAHEE	367
XXIV	WOMAN'S RIGHTS	374

CONTENTS

CHAPTER		PAGE
I	The Parody	11
II	When the Storm Winds Blow	30
III	Beginnings	50
IV	On the Trail	65
V	Burnaby's Cabin	87
VI	Gifts of Gratitude	99
VII	The Berry Patch	111
VIII	Doughnuts	130
IX	The Douglas Fir	146
X	Improvements	160
XI	"Brookside"	179
XII	Hunting	192
XIII	My Cabin	208
XIV	Christmas	221
XV	The Terror of the Forest	245
XVI	The Squatter	264
XVII	Up the Valley	277
XVIII	On the Peak	290
XIX	Hope Deferred Again	315
XX	Danger	323
XXI	When the Forests Burn	333
XXII	Fire and Water	349
XXIII	Illness	307
XXIV	Woman's Rights	374

ILLUSTRATIONS

PAGE

More useful so than a charred stub after
a fire . . . . *Frontispiece*

Material for a bonfire prepared by an avalanche 83

Such streams as these vanish when the forests
burn 161

The cool green depths of a Washington forest 282

"Whirlwinds of tempestuous fire" 333

The desolation after a fire 356

WHEN THE
FORESTS ARE ABLAZE

CHAPTER I

THE PARODY

THE sixteen teachers of the Whittier School leaned back in their chairs, chatting for a moment before they cleared away the fragments of their hasty luncheon. All but one had finished; she was devoted to Fletcherism.

"Is n't there any more tea?" she asked. "Can't you squeeze the handle a little hard—"

"To marry or not to marry; that is the question—"

Sally Brooks's clear, mocking voice could be heard above the hum of talk. The teachers laughed and listened. Sally's ready wit and clever parodies had lightened many a day's work.

[11]

"To be engaged! To marry,
             'T is a destination
Devoutly to be wished. To say 'Yes!' To be engaged!
Engaged! Perchance to be jilted. Aye, there's the rub:
To be left standing at the rose-embowered altar
While the recreant groom flees with another girl."

Handclaps and a chorus of laughter greeted the speaker.

"Sally's parodies are so clever," said Helen Stone to her neighbor, Jane Myers. But the laughing eyes widened with surprise as she glanced at her companion's face.

"Oh, yes, they're always fun," stammered Miss Myers, uncomfortably aware of the keen gaze searching her face. She had laughed and applauded with the others. She could not help it if her face flushed. The room was warm.

Miss Baker, from across the table, was also looking at her curiously. But a moment later there was the scraping of chairs on the bare floor as the teachers not on duty that week for "clearing up" passed in groups out of the room.

"*Did* you see Jane Myers's face?" asked Miss Baker, as the door closed behind the others. "You pile up the teacups and I'll look after the spoons and other things."

"Yes," answered Miss Bridges, "and I heard Sally Brooks's tone."

"You don't suppose she could have—"

"Who could have?"

"Oh, Sally—no, I mean Miss Myers."

"Could have what?"

"Oh, nothing. There—I knew you had piled those too high."

"Oh, dear. There's the bell! Why, that can't be right. We have at least ten minutes yet."

"No, we have n't. Parodies take time," and with a quizzical look on her face, Miss Baker dropped the silver and fled to her class room.

In the upper hall the sixth and seventh grade teachers had been talking.

"Oh, it could n't be! Sally is n't careful about hurting people's feelings, but she could n't have meant it. She is too much of a lady for that."

"But Miss Myers's face!"

"Ye-es. But there might have been some co-incidence."

Jane Myers's face was burning as she stood at her desk while the gong sounded and the lines of marching children filed into the room. She hoped they, at least, would not give her the searching glances she had received from two or three teachers. Yet children do have an uncanny way of seeing everything they are not expected to see.

"To marry or not to marry—"

The words rang through her head as she tapped her bell for the geography class.

"Engaged! Perchance to be jilted—"

"Johnnie, what is geography?"

Could Sally Brooks have known? Johnny was considering his question.

"Jogifry is round like an orange."

"What?"

"Yes 'm. It 's flat at the top an' bottom an' bulges out 'round the middle."

Jane explained carefully the trifling difference between the shape of the earth and jogifry.

"To be left standing at the rose-embowered altar—"

"Gilbert, give three reasons for saying the earth is round." Gilbert paused thoughtfully for a moment.

"While the recreant groom flees with another girl."

"Teacher says it 's roun' an' the book says it 's roun' and a man tole me it was roun'." Gilbert was triumphant. No theorem in geometry could have been more conclusively proved.

"Why, no. Now, Gilbert, your father is a sailor. Suppose he started to sail around the earth. Could he keep on sailing in the same direction until he came back to his starting point?"

"Nope," said Gilbert.

"Why not?"

" 'Cos he 's sick."

The door opened and Mrs. Fagan, shabby, untidy, half-frightened and wholly defiant, marched indignantly to the teacher's desk.

"I wants to know," she demanded in a loud voice, "why you never ups my bhoy?"

"You are Mrs. Fagan?"

"Shure, I 'ze Mrs. Fagan. Who else should I be? You ups all the ither bhoys and you does n't up my bhoy?"

The children were staring.

"Will you go to the principal, please, or else wait? I will be free in about five minutes."

"Wait for ye? Niver! I wants to know why ye did n't up my bhoy."

"I shall have to ask you to go to the principal. He will explain the matter."

Mrs. Fagan insisted. Miss Myers declined. By the time the irate woman had left the schoolroom was in a buzz of excitement.

Jane tapped the bell for quiet. There was little response.

"Silence, please." The tone was firm but one penetrating whisper continued.

"Silence!" There was silence then but discipline for the afternoon was done for. Even without Mrs. Fagan, her own disquiet with regard to Sally Brooks's parody left her without her usual control of the children.

There was little more information to be gleaned from the interrupted geography lesson. Sadie Brown insisted that a hemisphere is the thing that gives different kinds of heat, while Jim Blaker insisted with great positiveness that a blizzard was something inside of a hen.

The reading class droned over pioneer adventures—the romantic story of the Hudson's Bay Company retold in simple form.

"Why were the Hudson's Bay forts so important in the early pioneer days, Alice?"

" 'Cos the Injuns walked,—oh, ever so far, through the woods, to change their hides."

The afternoon wore on. During the writing lesson, that penetrating whisper again reached Jane.

"Still talking, Pearl."

"I told Elsie pa had his new teef. The top 'uns is all right but the bottomers teeter a leetle."

With indescribable relief Jane saw the children go that afternoon—even Jim Blaker who took advantage of "teacher's" very evident preoccupation to forget he had been kept in for fifteen minutes.

When the last one was fairly out and gone, Jane turned back to her desk. There was a pile of papers to be corrected, there was the next day's work to be prepared—and there was Sally Brooks to be considered. For the moment Sally had her entire attention.

Could it have been a mere coincidence? Jane thought over every detail of the circumstance. Sally's voice had been so full of meaning. But where could she have learned it? None of the teachers, so far as she knew, had acquaintances in the little Connecticut town where it all happened. And it was ten years ago! If Sally knew, had she told any of the others? Some had laughed—well, rather too heartily. And certainly some of them had given her very searching glances. Every trifle assumed great importance.

She picked up her pile of papers after a while, hoping to get away unseen. The clock pointed to a quarter to five. Perhaps they had gone.

No such luck! At the outer door a group of three were talking together. Of course they were talking of her! She was sure of that by the quick glances thrown at her, and they seemed to have changed the subject.

"Are n't you going home? Wait a minute," said Miss Stone as she tried to slip by them with a nod. Jane turned.

"I have some errands to do first. I 'll see you at dinner."

She walked hurriedly out of the yard and down the street. She was sure the teachers were looking after her. A block away she stopped with a jump. What a mistake! Why had she avoided them! She ought to have joined them and talked along as usual. If they did suspect

anything, she had given them grounds for it.
To be so embarrassed was to convict herself.
Oh, bother! Well, it was too late now. She
would have to be unusually lively at dinner.

Jane started off again and had walked a half
mile before she suddenly realized it was sprinkling. Then came the heavier rain. Raining—
no umbrella—and her best hat. It all came
back in a flash. She had intended to stop for
tea with the minister's wife on her way home,
therefore her best hat. But the umbrella was
locked in the empty schoolhouse. Harder and
harder down came the rain—the wet, pelting
rain of the east. The call was omitted of necessity and the rapid steps were turned toward the
boarding house. Jane reached it in no pleasant
temper.

Dinner at Mrs. Stone's was never an
hilarious meal. The boarders were all grade-
school teachers with the tendency, usual in any
grouping of this kind, to talk shop. To-night
the atmosphere was oppressive. One had been
reprimanded by her principal, another was
fagged by the day's grind, Jane was still cross
over the hat and the parody, and even Miss

Stone seemed to be in rather a "pecky," critical mood, with watchful eyes upon Jane. Yet, true to her resolution of the afternoon, Jane tried to be lively. Her keen sense of humor usually prevailed when the atmosphere was as deadly dull as to-night, but for once she failed. The amusing answers of the children, told without her usual spirit, fell flat.

Dinner was getting to be a nightmare when Barb Allen suddenly opened the door and came in like a cyclone.

"Hello! Did n't mean to be late! Oh, Miss Myers, here's a letter for you. Guess you did n't see it."

Jane looked at the unfamiliar postmark. It was from somewhere in Colorado. Then she opened it.

"Oh, girls! It's from Hope Denham. She's taken up a homestead!"

"A *homestead!*"

"Is she crazy?"

"Where is she?"

A half dozen questions and exclamations broke the dullness. Here was something doing.

"She's out West. Oh, you know she said last spring after she had that row with Mr. Mc-Fadden that she'd never teach again. She says she's having the grandest time."

"Why, what—"

"Read it, *please*."

"All right."

"Dear Jane:

What do you suppose Mac would say if he could see me here! It's awfully jolly. Just think of doing what you please all the time— all day long, keeping house for yourself in the dandiest log cabin—only the wood rats get in and that affects the jolliness sometimes,—and the mice! And then splitting your own wood and making garden and all that and yet making more money than teaching those awful young-'uns. I've got a hundred and sixty acres of land —all my own—some of it with trees on it and some of it bare. And the cutest little brook you ever saw though it dries up late in the summer. I just love it. I've been here four months now and I think that is a good test, don't you? I have only to wait five years until I prove up on it. And while I am waiting all I have to do is just to stay here and watch the minutes flock by. When my five years are up I 'll be worth a thousand dollars or more and have all the fun besides. Uncle Mart lives about two miles away and there 's another teacher who has taken up a claim on the next quarter section, though our cabins are about a quarter of a mile apart. She is doing it for her health. She has been here a year and she says she 's awfully tired of it. But I shall never be tired. I 'd rather do anything than teach school, especially after —! Uncle Mart gave me the dearest little Indian pony—though sometimes he does try to scrape me off. And I 'm learning to shoot— like anything. I have my own gun, too. I 'm having the grandest time. Whoop! Be sure to give my love to Mac. And why don't you take up a homestead instead of teaching everlastingly?

"Your shouting friend
"HOPE DENHAM."

"P. S. I forgot to say that last year Uncle Mart wrote me that if I 'd come out West, he 'd get me a homestead claim. There's another good one about five miles west of me, not taken up yet. Come out and join the pioneers. Do come, Jane.   H. D."

"That sounds just like her!"

"Are you going out there? Would you take up a claim?"

"Who is Mac?" asked one of them. And woman-fashion, all began to talk at once, with Barbara Allen in the lead.

"Mac was her principal—Mr. McFadden. They said she had an awful row with him—about the floors, wasn't it?"

"About several things, they say. But it started with the floors and her dress—don't you remember the fate of the blue one?"

"Oh, yes. When she came back in the fall a year ago, Hope had a pretty Alice-blue suit that she wore to school—but you know those oiled floors and what they would do to a nice skirt! Hope wore that suit and sent it to the cleaners again and again until the oil and the cleaning took all the color out of it around the bottom, besides the expense. Then she turned

[23]

sensible. Hope always was on strained rela-
tions with her salary, you know,"—Barbara Allen was excited now and talking without a
pause, at the top of her voice. The oiled floor
grievance was one which struck at all of them—
"so she got a dark gray dress for winter and wore
that. And there was one eleven-year-old girl
in her class who complained to her mother that
she did n't like Miss Denham's gray dress—she
liked the blue one better. So that mother went
straight to Mr. McFadden and told him that
teachers should be a model to their pupils and
that her daughter's taste in dress was being injured by the dreadful dress Miss Denham was
wearing."

"Actually."

"Yes, indeed."

"Then that crazy man,—he was only lately
married, or he 'd have known better,—why he
went straight to Hope to see that dress himself.
He had n't noticed it before—but neither had he
noticed the blue suit. It was one of those
dreadful, dark days when everything looks ugly,
and Hope had a north room, and the dress *did*
look dark. So he told her she ought not to wear

such ugly colors to school—that it affected the taste of the children."

"And Hope had tried to please the man by wearing that blue suit until it was ruined! That was too much for her! She told him she'd ruined one dress trying the educate the color-sense of the children, but so long as the school board persisted in using that horrid oil on the floors so it ruined every pretty dress she put on, she'd wear any dark old color she wanted to."

"She told him she'd wear crape if she wanted to," supplemented Miss Stone, "and that she felt like putting it on when she thought of that ruined blue suit."

"Oh, yes, they say they had an awful row. Hope reminded him that she was receiving the munificent sum of seven hundred and fifty per year—after he told her she ought to have at least two good school suits a year."

"That finished her career, of course."

"Oh, yes. He refused to reappoint her and told her he would never recommend her to any principal. She understood that she was favorably considered on two applications—Hope really was a good teacher, you know, and with her high spirits the children adore her—but he reported against her. Said her influence over the children was not good."

"Too bad!"

"Of course she ought n't to have 'sassed' him so."

"But it was n't fair."

"It 's as fair as lots of other things teachers have to put up with. Of course she ought to have swallowed his criticisms and worn a white shirt waist once in a while, or a red waist,—or something—but she was so wrathy over that pretty blue suit."

"The real injustice," remarked one of the teachers as they rose from the table, "lies in the fact that he was not an experienced teacher himself, nor a really capable man. He owed his position chiefly to the fact that he was of the masculine persuasion."

"Let 's all pull out and take up homesteads," said one tired-looking girl. "I 'm tired of teaching. There 's nothing in it."

Jane stood surveying the ruined hat a quarter of an hour later when there was a rap at the door.

"Come in. Oh, it 's you, Mrs. O'Brien."

The Irish washerwoman, big, fat, kind-hearted, lumbered in. She stood looking about her abstractedly, the big clothes basket at her feet. She was not usually so silent.

"It 's been a rainy day for you, has n't it?" said Rachel kindly.

"Yis." Silence again.

"An' it 's bad luck fer ye to-day, Miss Myers," she at last blurted out.

"It 's bad luck all around for me to-day, Mrs. O'Brien. What 's the matter now?"

Mrs. O'Brien stooped down and pulled away the newspaper covering the basket. Slowly she pulled out a dainty drawn-work shirtwaist with three great holes burned in the sheer lawn and in the delicate thread work.

"Oh!" gasped Jane in dismay. "How did it happen?"

"An' shure I be sorry," was the regretful answer.

"Oh, dear! Oh, dear!"

The drawn work represented a full summer's work, and the waist was Jane's main dependence. A French laundry might not have burned this waist, but it had lost entirely another nice waist a few months before, and Jane after that had preferred to trust the old Irish woman.

Mrs. O'Brien lifted out one piece after another, laying each on the couch full of pillows. On a long white skirt the embroidery of the flounce showed two big holes. A pretty cross-bar underwaist had a big black burn between the shoulders.

The explanation was simple enough when the old washerwoman found her tongue, and between voluble regrets Jane understood that Mrs. Mulaney's "chimbley" had caught fire and the pieces of burning soot had fluttered down on the clothes on the line next door.

But neither her own regret nor the volubility of Mrs. O'Brien helped matters much. School work was thrown aside in sheer disgust and the rest of that evening Jane spent in mending and darning, her mind full still of Sally Brooks and the day's mishaps.

Hair-brushing that night was a solemn affair when bedtime came. In between the long strokes of the brush, Jane looked at the burned clothing and the ruined hat. "Oh, this question of dress on a small salary," she said impatiently. "What a day it has been!"

She braided her hair with a frown.

"Oh, cheer up, Jane," she said suddenly, as she caught sight of her own reflection. "It might be a good deal worse."

"But just the same, Jane, my dear," she added as she turned out the light and raised the window, listening for a moment to the dashing rain without, "just the same, there's nothing in teaching. And if your lane does n't turn pretty soon, we will take up a homestead, because our finances are too much like a kitten chasing its tail,—it's impossible to make the two ends meet."

She fell asleep dreaming of homesteads, of vast plains and then of deeply forested mountains, with a vision of steady-footed pack horses toiling up the trail.

CHAPTER II

WHERE THE STORM WINDS BLOW

TWO months later Jane Myers brushed her hair and turned out her light in a different frame of mind, though the kitten was chasing its tail as energetically as ever. Her principal had called her to his office that day and offered her a position, for which he had been asked to recommend some one, as principal of the grade school of La Casa, Colorado.

"It may be lonely for you," he said as he studied the young woman before him, and noted with admiration the small bunch of violets which she wore, "but it is a distinct advance not only in position but in salary. It pays $1100. And it is a healthy place. I know physicians who send patients there—though there is no scenery. It is right out on the plains."

She had given him no definite answer then, though she answered herself quite promptly. "Of course we will do it, Jane, because that kit-

ten's activity bothers us. We can stand it for
a few years."

Since the parody, Jane's interest in the school
in which she had taught had dropped. The
teachers might or might not talk about her,
speculate about her, or say anything they chose.
When she had pulled herself together again, she
did not much care whether the parody was a
mere coincidence or not. But it had broken
into the cordiality of her feeling toward them.

So September came and with it Jane's new
work in La Casa. Inside of twenty-four hours
she understood and sympathized with the story
of a young man which had been told her by en-
couraging friends. Times had been hard and
he had been out of a position for some weeks,
until he was offered one at that town, with free
railroad fare. He arrived there at eleven
o'clock in the morning and left on the return
train at three that afternoon, paying his own
fare home.

Jane understood it perfectly, and she promptly
buried herself in her work as much as she could,
looking after school books, supplies of all kinds,
learning the names and qualifications of her

teachers, and thoroughly glad of all the absorbing minutiæ of the first days of the school year. So it was in sheer desperation that, when she met Miss Potter upon leaving school one afternoon of the first week, she suggested that they take a walk.

"Yes, indeed," said Miss Potter. "It is so beautiful." Miss Potter looked up in enthusiasm at the new principal. She had lived in that town all her life, and except for two years at the normal school, knew nothing of the world outside of it. She "adored" Miss Myers, she had told the third grade teacher that afternoon. And the third grade teacher had smiled and said, "I feel surprised every time she looks at me. She ought to have brown eyes, not violet ones."

"Don't you love it here?" asked Miss Potter as they started off from the school yard. And Jane, in the companionship of the cordial little soul whose western breeziness was like the fresh mountain air which swept over the plains, was conscious of some lightening of the blank gray homesickness which she was fighting. "In which direction shall we go?"

"Let's walk to the plains," said Jane, and both laughed. To the north lay the plains, to the south, to the east and to the west. Green with a recent rain, they stretched out endless, boundless, limitless. Not a house, not a tree, not a shrub—absolutely nothing was there to break that immensity carpeted with short green grass and the low broad leaves of the cactus. Toward the west, beyond the range of vision, lay the barrier of the Rocky Mountains. The open sweep of the plains was glorious, yet she longed to see that distant purple barrier. If they were only near enough so that she could see the setting sun sink behind the mountains, deep blue shadows at their base, and the rosy tinting of the snowy peaks!

"Let's walk on," suggested Jane after they had passed the half mile of plank walks and the long rows of little one-story houses which lay between the school and the edge of the town where houses and sidewalks suddenly ended and the level plains began. There was nothing in the town to explore. Plank sidewalks flanked by the low houses arranged in parallel rows with cross streets at proper intervals—that was all. In the center of the town was a tiny park, one block square, fringed with quivering-leaved cottonwood trees. Around the square were the stores and larger buildings of the town. Beyond the houses, in every direction, lay the eternal flatness.

"Isn't it beautiful? Don't you love it?" asked the enthusiastic Miss Potter. She looked up in admiration at the woman beside her. Wavy hair Ruth Potter had always admired— hair that waved just enough to be fluffy and roll back from the face. Her own, a lifelong grievance, was an uncertain brown, straight as an Indian's, and no amount of crimping papers nor even a curling iron would make it roll back as it should from the plain face whose one beauty was its happy expression.

"It is wonderful—wonderful, in its own way. It has a distinctive beauty of its own but I love the mountains." She looked out over the sweep of green to the far-off horizon from which the softening light of dusk was creeping. From somewhere out in that shadowy light came the song of the meadow lark, sweetest of

all singers. Again and again from the fading
light came the soft, sweet trill. There were
no shadows on the plains to slip along stealthily
in the twilight, one creeping behind another,
taking their places secretly, silently, here behind
a bush or stone, there behind a tree, or under
the shelter of waving grass, or among the rushes
by a riverside. There was nothing in all that
vast expanse to cast a shadow. Only the lessening of the light, the gradual dimming of the
plain, the deepening of the blue autumn mist in
the vast distances,—and then suddenly the dark
had crept up around the two girls standing out
there alone on the shadowy plain. The song of
the lark had ceased.

As they returned to the town, Miss Potter
chatted cheerfully as they passed the houses
from which lights were twinkling. Here lived
Tommy Jones who had given them so much
trouble the year before,—yonder was the house
where the former principal boarded,—there
lived Lizzie Wilson who was the brightest little girl in the town,—all the endless talk of
a small town. But Jane heard little. The

[35]

beauty of the plains she had seen had for the moment banished homesickness. If there were only some mountains in sight!

Many another walk the two teachers took that fall, before the November rains came and the winter snows. October brought days when the air was fresh and clear, invigorating as air can only be when it is blown straight down through a sunny sky from snow-capped mountain peaks. There was nothing in the shaking, quivering, yellow leaves of the cottonwoods to give even a touch of color to the town, though they reminded Jane of the autumn glory of her old New England home, but the plains were something entirely new with their endless sweep of green, and high over head the broad blue dome which fitted down over the great green flatness.

"A man could hide behind nothing except his own shadow out here," Jane had remarked one day. To which Miss Potter had answered, "But on a baking summer day he could n't do even that."

Then the cold rains of autumn came, and bridge, embroidery, books, or even mending, was better than a cold walk in the mud, or the dreary trudging along the plank walks, with the bleak plains outstretched before her and a heavy gray sky above her. Jane took no more walks.

And after winter came, with its high winds and deep snows, the walk to and from school was more than many of the teachers cared for.

Bleak and cold and white, covered deep with snow, lay the endless plains. So far as the eye could reach stretched that boundless sheet of unbroken white, grim and somber under the gray skies, blinding in its whiteness on sunny days. And in the penetrating sunlight every ugly line in the houses of the shabby little town was shabbier, every ungraceful curve flaunted itself. Brilliant, cruel, merciless, the sunshine seemed almost an enemy. The sky above was a blue bowl of intense, hard blue, not the soft radiant blue of a summer sky. Jane liked better the days when the skies were gray, but that meant more snow, and still more snow, piled in white masses through the streets by the winds.

There was little to interest in the town—no music, no theater, unless one might misuse the

term for a cheap moving picture show, no art,
no lectures, few people of education or refine-
ment except an occasional homesick invalid,
and nothing whatever to inspire a homesick
teacher.

She found that teaching was no more congenial when supervising the work of other teachers, than it was when doing the work herself.
In some ways it was more discouraging to see
others do so badly what she knew she herself
could have done well. Some of the teachers
were oversensitive to even the kindliest criticisms, and, as is usually the case, they were the
ones who needed them most.

"It's no use," she said one day just before
Christmas, as she put on her wraps. "I was
never born to be a teacher and neither was I
born to be smothered in the awful slowness of a
small, sordid town. Give me the city or else
give me the depths of a forest. I am sure I
don't want the plains. This betwixt and between is too awful."

The glaring light of the plains dazzled her,
and the keen, penetrating sunlight had no in-
spiration for her as she turned toward the post

office. She had had no mail for a week for all trains were snow-bound in the high drifts. Probably the outgoing mail would be as badly delayed as the incoming, yet she felt if she could send off her Christmas letters and packages that the dating stamp would explain any possible delay.

The general store, one side of which was occupied by the post office, was crowded with women making their Saturday purchases, and with an idle throng of men leaning against barrels or perched on boxes. She waited her turn at the window impatiently, conscious of a strong repugnance to the crowd in the store. Finally the clerk took her package and weighed it, while several idlers watched her.

"Any mail for me?" she asked.

"No mail fur enny body, Miss Myers. Trains all late."

Jane felt rather than saw an idler near her start as her name was given. As she turned to go their eyes met. He recognized her in a flash, but it took her a second to recognize the dissipated face and shifty eyes of this man in the loud-checked suit. For an instant she was

[39]

too stunned to move. The man mistook her start.

"Why—er—hello," he said, half offering a dirty hand.

Without even a glance, Jane turned and passed out of the store, followed by the curious gaze of the entire crowd.

Panic-stricken, yet white-hot with anger, eyes flashing and lips compressed, the principal struggled up the snowy street to her boarding house. Once in her room, she faced her reflection in the glass. Then she spoke firmly.

"This ends any possibility, Jane, of your keeping this position. Next year you will be somewhere else than in La Casa. Now don't let me hear another word about this. Do you understand?"

One might readily have thought she was talking so sternly to something else than a reflection in a mirror.

The talk at dinner that night drifted to ranch life and homesteading. The landlady had a guest who had taken up a quarter section near the mountains and was developing a fine ranch. Her son had taken up the adjoining

homestead so they worked the two places together.

"They's lots er wimmen doin' it," she as-
serted, "and making money out of it. My
ranch ain't cost me nuthin' 'cept living on it five
years and a little stock, and I reckon I'm wuth
two or three thousand dollars now. Ye
could n't make thet in five years teachin' school,"
she added, turning to Jane.

"I should think not," was Jane's prompt
answer. "I'm so tired of teaching that I've
sometimes thought of taking up a homestead
myself—that is, thought of it vaguely. It's a
wild idea for me, I'm afraid."

"An' why is it wild? I done it."

"I don't like the plains. I get tired of the
flatness. I'd want to be up in the mountains,
among the trees."

"Sure. Mis' Lawson, she took up a homestead on a timber claim. She reckons her
timber's worth about three thousand dollars.
She jes' sat down on it fur five years—but she
war n't really thar mor 'n two."

"She could n't do that now, could she—without commuting? You see," Jane added, "I

have a friend who has taken up a homestead and she's written me a good deal about it."

"Guv'ment's stricter now—some stricter," answered her landlady.

"You'd have to live there now, would n't you, to prove up on it?"

"A little, mebbe—but shucks!"

"Is it really possible," asked Jane after a few moments' thought, "for a woman to take up a homestead in the forest and live there for five years—and do it in safety?"

"Sure. Did n't I jes' tell you 'bout Mis' Lawson? Ain't I done it? Course I'm on the plains, but she's in the timber."

Jane brushed out her hair that night in a very thoughtful mood. The approach of Christmas made her homesick, and the far-reaching stretches of endless white depressed her. The children and teachers were restless, planning for the holidays, and a spirit of unrest pervaded the air. The situation had been doubtful enough, but the sudden appearance of Ed Brent had ended any possibility of staying in La Casa. "And I am so tired of teaching," she sighed as she slipped into bed.

"Miss Myers," said Ruth Potter in a frightened tone one evening as they bundled up for the walk home, "who is that man?"

"What man?"

"The one who hangs around the school so much?"

"I have n't seen him. I don't know. What sort of looking man? What does he do?"

Jane suddenly wished she were only a teacher, with a man principal.

"I don't know. He just hangs around. There he is!"

Jane turned quickly, only to see the vague outlines of a man walking in the other direction.

"It 's too dark to see clearly. He is probably the father of some of the children."

"I don't believe so," said Miss Potter decidedly. "But I can't see what he wants."

There was a well-defined fear in Jane's mind as to who the man might be.

"Suppose you wait for me," she said after a moment, "so that we always walk home together. He 'd hardly address two women—if that 's what he is up to."

A blizzard was more serious than "something

[43]

inside of a hen," Jane thought one February night as she left the schoolhouse alone. She had stayed later than usual and Miss Potter had gone at noon. She bent her head to the wind, pulling down her fur cap as far as it would come over her hair, and buried her face in her fur collar. But still the snowy needles stung her face and filled her eyes. It was half past five, and dark except for the light of the snow. The day at school had been a miserable one. The high wind had blown in a west window and had frightened the children half to death. None had been hurt,—she was thankful for that. Though one or two had been struck by the flying glass, still the only damage had been slight cuts in their clothing. But it had taken hard work to put away the books and supplies, blown all over the room by the wind, until the janitor could nail boards over the window.

She hurried along through the deep snow, stepping aside from the drifts, noting little in the storm until she became conscious through some alert sense, that she was being followed. She remembered, now that she thought of it, as she turned the corner near the school she had

seen a man on the other side of the street. She
hurried on, floundering through the storm, conscious that he was coming closer and closer until she turned the corner near her boarding
house. He would hardly follow her farther.
It was only a moment then until she opened the
door and was greeted by friendly voices.

"Come in. We've been saving the warmest
corner for you."

"Let me take off your coat."

"No school, to-morrow. That's sure. The
children can never get through this blizzard."

In the warmth and friendliness, Jane put
aside her fears. The idea of any man following her through such a storm! It was probably
some one who lived near and had to come her
way.

"The bean soup is burned, but I can't help it,"
declared her landlady at dinner. "This new
girl's got a follower, and her head's thet
turned!"

"Miss Myers had a follower to-night. See if
her head is turned," laughed one of the teachers.

Jane started. "Was that man following me?"

she demanded a little sharply, "or was he just coming up this street?"

"He was following you, Miss Myers," said the teacher, more seriously. "He was close behind you and when he saw where you turned in, he tried to see the number of the house. It was under the snow, of course. Then he looked up and down the street as though trying to fix the location in his mind."

"Miss Myers has made a hit," laughed another, seeing that Jane was a little alarmed.

"I don't like being followed," Jane protested. "It frightens me."

"I think it is that man who has been hanging around the school, Miss Myers."

"There's no occasion for alarm," said Mrs. Graham kindly, as she poured out the muddy coffee.

"But any man who'd follow a woman eight blocks through such a storm as this—he must have some motive." Jane was thoroughly alarmed.

"I saw him one day—if he's that man that I've met once or twice near the school," said one of the teachers. "I think his name is Brent.

He's a professional gambler, Jim Howard told me once. He pointed him out. Miss Myers, if he bothers you, Jim Howard will settle him. Jim's afraid of nobody. He can lay out any man in town."

"If he ever does address me," said Jane gratefully, "believe me, I'll be only too glad to have your Mr. Howard 'lay him out.' "

After dinner in her own room a few weeks later, Jane sat writing letters. One was to Hope Denham, and a few sentences in it read as follows:

"I can't stand teaching school another year. Your example has unsettled me for this life of grind, and as soon as school is out in the spring, I am coming to visit you. I find it is not by any means impossible for a woman to take up a homestead in the forest, and I have written Sue Fairfax to ask Bert to select some sort of a claim for me in the Northwest. I would rather be in Washington, I think, than in Idaho or Oregon. They live in Spokane and I think I should feel nearer to them if I were in the same state."

But to Sue Fairfax, after a discussion of homesteads and homesteading, Jane wrote:

"So you see, Sue, I cannot stay here another year. He never spoke to me but he followed me until I was nearly wild. Then a Mr. Howard, a raw-boned young giant, engaged to one of the teachers, warned him that if he followed me again or endeavored to speak to me, that he would thrash him thoroughly. Since then, he has left me alone. I am not afraid of him, Sue, you know, but I feel disgraced. Not that he jilted me as he did—how thankful I am he did,—but that he has it in his power to say that he was once engaged to me! You can see where that would put the principal in a petty town like this! I am nearly worn out from the nervous strain of my own fears. And, anyway, I could not stay in this joyless town. For six weeks in the fall it is glorious. Then it's heavy rains, with streets bottomless in mud, high winds, blizzards and snow, *snow!* In the spring it is melting snow, flooded streets, water to your shoe tops, more bottomless pits of mud, fearless gales, a few glorious days, and then warm weather. If one

[48]

could live on an elevated platform and escape the snow and water and mud, there are seasons which would be beautiful, but you can't see sunshine with bedraggled skirts and soaking feet. And this Brent business settles it all. So I want Bert to get me a homestead. I 'm going to visit Hope Denham as soon as school is out, and then I am coming to visit you, my twin. You 've invited me often enough, but I have always been clear across the continent."

CHAPTER III

BEGINNINGS

SPOKANE, August 17.

Dear Hope:

Here I am, so far on my way, thanks to your example and encouragement. But if you could hear the opposition of the Fairfaxes! Bert and Sue both knew all about that broken engagement ten years ago, and yet Bert turned to me with a calm:

"Jane, why don't you marry? You used to be the belle of the town."

Is n't that just like a man? I told him that I had had my day, that I had been disillusioned, and that I wanted to live my own life. But the conversation went right around in a circle,—this way:

Bert: "But I cannot see why a young, good-looking woman should want to bury herself on a homestead."

[50]

Jane: "I'm not so very young.   I'm nearly twenty-nine."

Bert indignantly: "I'm thirty-three and I call myself young."

Jane: "And I'm not particularly good look-ing, only my hair is wavy and my eyes don't match my complexion.   (I'm so tired of being told I ought to have brown eyes.)   And I have to earn my living somehow."

"I think you could get a good position in the schools here."

"I don't want to teach.   I'm tired of teach-ing."

"Jane, why don't you marry?"

"Because I don't want to.   I could never trust any man again."

"He was a cad.   You're wrong to mourn over that."

"*Mourn!*   When I think what a narrow es-cape I had it takes my breath away!"

Then Sue would break in: "Jane, dear, you'd be so much happier married."

"Men like Bert don't grow on every bush, you know.   I don't want to marry."

Sue: "And you admit you have refused two eligible men in the last five years?"

Jane: "Yes—because I want to live my own life."

Bert, in a horrified tone: "Heavens! You 're not one of these woman's rights women, are you?"

He looked so disgusted.

Jane: "I 've given precious little thought to woman's rights. I don't care a rap about voting, but I want to live my own life. And I have a right to do it."

"What sort of men were these you refused?"

"Attractive, educated—every one spoke well of them. We were good friends—but that was all."

"They cared for you?"

"They were quite emphatic in their assertions."

"Be honest. Are n't you sorry you refused both of them?"

"No. Not a bit. I don't want to discuss marriage, please."

Then Bert would change his tactics. He must have had two hundred and twenty-seven friends who had taken up homesteads, judging from the stories he told me, and the more attractive the homestead, the greater the dangers. Then he would begin a front attack again:

"It's wild, utterly wild, Jane. If you were a farmer's daughter—"

Jane: "I am."

Bert: "I mean accustomed to heavy work and a rough life. Then it would be different. Then you might weather it. But think what it means for you, an educated, city-trained woman, to live in a rough log cabin in the forest, bringing in every bucket of water from a spring or a creek, breaking the ice in winter, perhaps, with wolves howling around your cabin at night, cougars screaming, snow ten to twenty feet, bear tracks all too evident—"

"I thought bears hibernated during the winter."

I had him there. Then I added.

"It will be the greatest fun to learn to walk on snowshoes. And if cougars roost in my trees I'll shoo them off. I'll go ski-ing down the hills at the rate of two miles a minute, and I'll—"

Bert: "I'm serious. Please talk sense."

Jane: "I'm serious, too. Other women take up homesteads."

"But—"

"And some of them are teachers."

"Yes, but—"

"Why can't I do what other women do—and glory in?"

"Because—"

"Didn't you read that article in this month's 'Northwestern' on 'Women Ranchers in the Northwest,'—and it gave photographs of the women, strong, happy, successful, too."

"Hang it! The chap who wrote that never saw a woman homesteader, I'll bet. Never was on a homestead—doesn't know what one looks like. You know how magazine articles are written."

"I intend to take up a homestead."

And that's the way the argument ended.

After I had gone to my room that night, though, Ted began to cry a little and I slipped into his room to quiet him. As I came into the hall—I had turned out the light because it was

moonlight—Bert and Sue came up the stairs. I
heard Bert say:

"Sue, it can't be that Jane is one of these awful, strong-minded women! Why, she talks like
a man hater! She'll be one of these woman's
rights women, first thing we know."

Sue said: "No-o. I could n't believe that of
Jane. I think she simply has n't met the right
man."

"She's likely to meet him on a homestead in
the forest, is n't she? Swede wood-chopper!
Humph! And if she takes up a homestead
she'll be there five years—until she is thirty-
three."

Sue's voice sounded a little worried.

"She might commute. She has that little
legacy from her mother and—"

Then their door shut.

You know, Hope, that I'm not a man hater,
though I went through enough with Ed Brent
to make me one. But I like men as comrades—as friends—and I have n't any intention
of marrying. Besides, I never, *never* could
stand it to have a man tell me what I could

or could not do. And neither would I ever marry a man who would let me do the bossing. I couldn't respect him. So it's better not to marry and perhaps land in a divorce court. I do not think I am really "strong-minded" though I know I seem very independent, because no woman can meet the world year after year and not have a little air of decision,—call it determination, if you like,—that she would not get in a sweet, happy home. But I *can't* stand dictation.

Bert wound up by writing to a friend of his, a mill owner in Illahee, asking him if there were any desirable homestead claims in his section. This Mr. Burnham wrote back that there was one. It had been taken by some Irishman while it was still outside the forest reserve, and then the reserve lines were extended and took him in, as well as an old lady who has the next claim and has already proved up on hers. Mr. Burnham said he could get the relinquishment for me before the new law goes into effect. Under the new law I could not do this. The frequent changes in laws and in the lines of the reserves are rather confusing, so they say. Anyway, I have this one extraordinary chance of getting a homestead claim if I want it, so I nabbed it.

I leave here the last of August for Tyee— that's a larger town—and I transfer to a local line which runs out to Illahee. It's just a saw-mill town among the forests and I know it will be very picturesque. Then for my homestead!

I had a beautiful visit with Sue. She certainly is happy and the children are little dears. I told you once, I think, that Sue and I were born on the same day in the same town, and our mothers were close friends, so Sue and I have always called ourselves twins. But just now she thinks I ought to get married. I don't.

Your friend,
JANE.

ILLAHEE, September 1.

Dear Hope:

I've been in this town just twenty-three hours, but I'm not nearly so sure about things as I was. I've got to do *something*—quick—so I am writing you.

I came to Illahee, via Tyee, and reached here last night—Saturday. That was a mistake, for

Sunday in a strange place is depressing. Mr. Burnham was to be here Monday morning, and I did n't want to come in Sunday evening, but how I wish I had!

I had engaged a room, but when I was shown it—the less said the better. It was exactly like the descriptions in novels of hotels in a frontier town. I thought the great American frontier was gone. Certainly the hotels have not. The building is a two-story frame, flush with the street except for a narrow, dirty, grimy, tobacco-juice-stained porch, which runs the length of the building. The shirt-sleeved men lounging in the chairs with feet on the railing were not in the least the traditional western heroes, and they stared at me until I blushed behind my veil. I gave my name and asked for my room and got another long stare from the clerk. He was also in shirt sleeves.

He took my suit case and walked up narrow, dirty stairs to the second story. A long hall ran from one end of the building to the other, bordered by rows of cells. I was given the corner one, with a view on a saloon on the side and a row of cheap stores opposite. And the room! No description could ever do justice to it. Now this is the truth. The walls were covered with faded blue paper, bright in tone in spite of the fading, with an immense sprawling vine on it. The ceiling, figured in big geometrical patterns, was of a bright purplish blue, and the carpet gloried in big red roses. Torn green shades at the low windows, with dirty white sash curtains—that completes the room. No, it does n't either, for the furniture was of that unspeakable cheap pine. It fairly made me dizzy to look at this complication of varying figures in two shades of blue with those big red roses. That's why I am writing you. If it were only Monday morning.

It was too warm to stay in the house to-day so I did start out this morning to go to church, but when I saw the dreary-looking place, I turned away and went on a walk.

The town nestles low between two mountains, east and west. On the south the hills are much lower, and to the north, or from the north, comes the Illahee river, winding down between the mountains. I walked to a point where I could see up the valley, blue with haze. One moun-

[59]

tain after another jutted out, forested from top to bottom, and far in the distance I could catch the top of a mountain tipped with snow. I'd be in sight of a mountain peak from my claim, I believe, if it were not that the forest cuts off my view.

Up and down the valley there was no sign of human habitation, or even the ax. The forests were as endless as the plains. But close to the town the trees have been cut, leaving great stretches bristling with ugly stumps and forlorn débris. I passed several such stretches of deforested land on my way out, and a more cheerless, depressing sight I never saw. The land had been "skinned," as they say, and simply left to go to ruin. There ought to be a law against such logging, for it ruins the country in every way. And besides, if a match happens to get in its work in such a mass of débris, or the sparks from an engine, the fire usually spreads into the standing timber, and makes a destructive blaze there besides killing off all the new growth on the land already cut. I'll believe anything I ever hear about the Americans being a wasteful people after what I 've seen of these "skinned" lands.

MONDAY EVENING.

Mr. Burnham came this morning, so I 'll add this to my letter of yesterday. I had a short talk with him in the close, hot, stuffy hotel parlor. He is very much a gentleman, very thoughtful and considerate. He is about Bert's age, rather small, wiry, dark hair, eyes nearly black, a very pleasant face, tanned very brown. I fancy he has a keen sense of humor. He told me all about my homestead. My cabin is being built as near as possible to Mrs. Patton's—the old lady who has proved up on her claim,—but there is a stream between. The cabin of the man from whom I bought the relinquishment was in a sort of natural meadow which forms about one-third of my hundred and sixty acres. He took the liberty, he said, of deciding upon the other location though it is right in among the trees, in order to have me near Mrs. Patton. That is just what I wanted, you know,—to be in among the trees. I am going out with him

Wednesday morning, though the cabin is not yet finished. He said Mrs. Patton would take me in.

After he went, with forty-eight hours of this ghastly idleness ahead of me, I started to explore the town. Everywhere it is as ugly as original sin. There is n't a picturesque thing about it. The crude rawness of the town, its roughly built shacks, stores with false fronts to give an impression of height, and the grim devastation immediately surrounding it—I never imagined there could be such force in that old saying that God made the country and man made the town.

The sawmills are just north of the town on the edge of a pond, or tiny lake, made by damming the river just under the clumsy, primitive log bridge. On one side of the bridge is the rippling river, though it is low now, but on the other is this quiet pond in which the logs float. The logs are enormous, but everything out here is on such a big scale. This afternoon I went over to the sawmill and watched the machinery. It was fascinating to follow the unbroken stream of sawdust and small bits of wood which fall from the conveyor on the great sawdust heap which burns day and night, year in and year out, sending up a cloud of thick, blue smoke. I like the fragrance of the burning wood, even if it is rather pungent. I kept out of the way of the belts, but it was the greatest fun watching them saw the big logs, five or six feet in diameter, into boards. They saw first on one side, then an iron arm, called the "nigger" turns the log over, until they almost square it. The music of the town is the whirl and hum and buzz of the flashing saws, with the occasional hissing of escaping steam. It was a busy picture and really very interesting.

I wandered over to the schoolhouse to see if I might scratch up an acquaintance with any of the teachers, but found that school did not open until next Monday. I shall spend to-morrow watching the sawmill, for lack of anything better to do, and my evening writing letters. Wednesday morning I'm off for the homestead. I feel much better since I met Mr. Burnham. The fact that he knows Bert makes me feel acquainted with him. He is part owner of one of the mills here.

Did I tell you the streets are paved with sawdust? Everything here has the fragrance of freshly sawed lumber.

Despite Bert's predictions, I know I am going to be happier on my claim than teaching school, and I feel so thankful to you for putting me in the notion of it.

With love,
JANE.

CHAPTER IV

ON THE TRAIL

"ARE you all right now?" asked Burnham. He had just finished shortening a stirrup for Jane, and he glanced up at her curiously as she sat a-top a small cayuse pony, not altogether certain whether or not the tricky little beast would allow her to finish her journey in safety. He gave a final pull to the cinch band, a final glance at the khaki-clad figure, and then sprang on his own horse.

"Your horse's name is Dempsey," he remarked.

"And yours?" She patted Dempsey's head.

"Bob. Now. All ready!"

"You are sure you have everything?" he asked again, as they turned away from the staring group on the porch.

"I think so."

"Your revolver 's in your saddle bag?"

"Yes. Will I need to take it out?"

"Not this morning. I have mine, you see. The bears have plenty of berries at this season and we are not likely to meet any other wild animals."

The soft thud of the ponies' feet resounded on the sawdust-paved streets as they turned toward the bridge. The golden glow of the dust struck out by her pony in the golden light of that morning in early September was a picture Jane never forgot.

Down the straggling street, bordered by the tiny log cabins or the one-story shacks of board, to the rough corduroy bridge which spanned the Illahee, they rode in silence. Jane paused a moment on the bridge. On one side was the rushing stream, still swirling and purling over the rocks, still managing to give an impression of white foam and of danger though the snows had long since melted in the summer sun. On the other side, in the pool formed by the crude dam, floated the logs, three to six feet in diameter, besides a few of smaller size. The chained logs which enclosed the boom floated lazily on the pond while the shriek of the saws and the humming of the great whirling belts broke the stillness. Blue smoke rose to-day as always, day and night, from the ever-burning heap of smoldering sawdust, though now and then the small ends carried by the conveyor lent a blaze to the pile.

Across the bridge was a good road, through a section where logging was still carried on. Far down below them, the donkey engine was dragging huge logs to the rollway, tumbling them with a mighty splash into the river, to be floated down to the mill.

They rode in silence for the first few miles, through the logged-off land and then in the forest. As the road suddenly rounded the shoulder of a mountain, they came in full view of the glorious peak, white with snow, shining against the deep blue sky above. Far below ran the silvery river, gleaming here and there between the dark sides of the densely forested lower mountains. As they paused to look through the fresh air came the acrid smoke of burning wood. There was a slight fire below them, around the mountain's shoulder. "Of no consequence," he said as he noticed her startled look. Then they rode on again. Shortly beyond, the road

ended and a trail began. Burnham talked a little now and then, but Jane was rather silent.
One fact stared her in the face; that she was now
taking what seemed to be an irrevocable step.
At any time during the preceding week she
could have sold her goods and returned to the
cozy home of Sue Fairfax. Now she was on
her way to her claim, twenty miles out from this
little sawmill town, and without a horse it
would be difficult to return. Was she making a
mistake? Was Bert Fairfax right? And Mr.
Burnham! She remembered how surprised he
was when he found she was going to take up a
homestead in the forest. He had even hinted
rather broadly that it was a risky thing for her to
do. But why risky for her if other women—
other teachers—did it?

"You are sure Mrs. Patton will not object to
my staying with her until my cabin is built?"
she asked suddenly.

"No, not at all. She is very glad to make a
little money by doing for those who happen
along in her direction—though that is chiefly
Goss and myself. Goss is forest ranger of this

district and his headquarters are several miles beyond Mrs. Patton's. When he is passing there, or comes in off a long trip he goes down there for meals. I have an old cabin beyond there, too." Then added a moment later, "Your cabin must be almost finished. The men were getting along on it all right when I came down."

"I appreciate your kindness," she said.

"Don't mention it. Fairfax is a good friend of mine." Again there was silence, broken by Burnham's comment. "You 'll meet Goss, I suppose. He is a king among men."

She glanced at the man beside her,—lean, browned by sun and wind, with dark, laughing eyes, a man who evidently loved the wood and the open air. He used good English, she noticed. Fairfax had said he was a man to be trusted, and he certainly had an open, frank face. Just then he was whistling.

"See that tree!" he said, suddenly interrupting himself.

"I can't very well help it." Jane halted her pony looking up at the giant which arose di-

rectly from the middle of the trail. Ten feet
in diameter, some thirty in circumference, towering two hundred and fifty feet straight into the
air, with not a branch nearer the ground than a
hundred feet.

"That's a king among trees certainly," she
said. The longer she looked at the tree the
mightier it appeared as its full circumference
and height bore in upon her.

"They did n't cut *that* down. The trail goes
around it. This is a ten mile point. Do you
want to get off and rest?" Burnham was not
in the least sure that this tenderfoot would last
the full twenty miles. "And if she does n't
what in thunder *will* I do?" he muttered.

Jane looked around her. The forest on either
side was dense. The sunlight hardly penetrated
the green crests of the tall firs. Tropical underbrush could hardly seem more of a jungle.
On a rising slope of the forest lay great trunks
flat upon the ground or half balanced over
other huge trunks, blown over by some storm,
or fallen by decay. One tall fir had in its fall
become wedged between two others, equally
large, but too close together to allow it to fall

[70]

to earth. There the great giant leaned, resting its full weight upon its sturdy supporters.

"I 'll rest a few moments," she said. Horseback riding was a new experience. Burnham took her hand and attempted to assist her. Jane forestalled his effort by an attempted light spring from the horse's back,—and landed on her knees at his feet.

"Are you hurt?" He helped her up.

"No-o, but I did n't know I was so stiff." She wobbled badly as she made her way to a flat stone by the trail. Burnham politely turned his back to her and led the horses to a near-by sapling. He could keep his face straight under any provocation, but he could not keep the laughter out of his eyes.

In a few moments he rejoined her.

"I thought this was all a forest reserve," remarked Jane breaking the silence. "How can you log in a reserve or take up a homestead, either?"

"These two homesteads were taken up before it was thrown into a reserve, and you bought Mullaney's relinquishment. You could n't take up a new homestead in here now—and that fact is going to make it more lonely for you, I am afraid. You will not have any other neighbors, you see, than Mrs. Patton. But as to the logging—that is chiefly carried on outside of the reserve."

"It's all the same forest—and the trees are just as large."

"Yes, but a reserve usually follows township lines and frequently does not include a good-sized tract of valuable timber. I don't know why the government does it in that way, but it does."

As they started on again, the open trail, such as it was, ended. Beyond the great fir there was barely a bridle path. Burnham took the lead and she followed closely, pushing the branches aside. Few trees had been cut at all on this trail—they were merely blazed. The underbrush had been hacked away close to the ground, but sometimes the luxuriant growth of the "jungle" almost filled the vacant space.

Burnham turned half-way in his saddle to talk to her. "There are look-out points along the other side of the river," he explained, "points which the forest guards visit every day during the summer for any traces of a fire. The views from some of them are wonderful."

"It's all wonderful," she breathed.

"Yes, it is." His own face lighted up. "And Goss is proud of his district. There's never been a bad fire in here."

"Fire!" The word seemed to come a little nearer home than when forest fires were discussed on a pleasant porch in Spokane.

"Yes, indeed. That is the hardest work of a forest ranger. But can you imagine," he added after a minute, "how little chance mere humans would have against a fire in this forest?"

Jane shivered, but not altogether because the air was damp and moist, almost chilly, under these great trees though out in the sunshine it was warm enough.

The broad, coarse leaves of the thimble berry and the shining, waxen leaves of the salal brushed her stirrups. Even the sharp-pointed leaves of the Oregon grape were tall enough to attract her attention. The berries were just ripe and here and there a cluster of the purple grapes caught her eye. Some of the leaves were already turning crimson. The underbrush became more and more impenetrable. Great mossy, decaying logs, of enormous size and length lay about on the ground, almost hidden by the jungle of bushes and wild growth which rioted over them. At one point the trail led under an uprooted log and though she had to flatten herself out on her horse, they passed without dismounting under it. But again and again the trail had turned to go around such fallen giants.

Burnham's cheery whistle, the *thud* of the horses' feet and the rustling of leaves and swish of branches as they passed were the only sounds which broke the silence. There might be birds in the great dim stretches of the woods but she did not see them.

"Are there Indians in here?" she asked suddenly.

"Yes, a few. They are not dangerous, though. But let me warn you," he added suddenly, "if you ever do meet Indians, *never* let them see that you are afraid of them. An Indian despises anything which is afraid and the moment you show fear you find yourself in

[74]

their power. And *never* go outside your cabin door without firearms."

"What Indians are they?"

"Some who have refused to go on reservations. They live in the woods and along the streams, going and coming as they please. You might live here ten years and never see one. Or you might encounter a number in the first week. They shoot game out of season, though, and that bothers the rangers. And they set fires, too, if it suits their convenience. Goss would sleep better if there were no Indians in his district."

The trail began to wind downward, through the dim arches of the trees.

"Just what is the work of a ranger?" asked Jane.

"Everything to do with the forests under their care. They see that squatters do not cut the timber, that fires are reported and fought, that the game laws are observed, that the sheep men pay their fees and do not graze except where they're allowed to, and they try to get rid of all predatory animals. Of course, they do not get rid of them all, but seventy-five timber wolves

[75]

were killed in this district last winter by his guards."

"And the fires!"

"From April until November they are always on the lookout for fires—unless the snows come early. They put out the little ones and try to divert the big ones. Do you want a drink of water?"

In the downward turn, they had come to the banks of the Illahee—come to it suddenly, out of the cool dimness. Spanned by a narrow, unguarded bridge, the blue river just below them ran smoothly now, for it was fall and all the streams were low, though Jane could readily imagine the rush of the wide stream in its spring flood. On both sides rose the densely forested hills, peaks towering above her into the blue, and on the topmost peaks a sprinkling of snow which had fallen in the night.

Burnham slipped off his horse and dipped up a cup of water from a stream trickling down to the river. It was clear and cool. She drank it mechanically. The river, the mountains, the forest held her attention. She was in the heart of the forest—and she knew the meaning of the phrase now. No one ever realizes it until he has been in the forests' depths.

"The bridge?" she asked, as Burnham sprang on his pony again.

"It is the only bridge over the Illahee except at the mills. Any one wanting to cross that river, unless he can ford it far above, must cross here. It was built for the fire service."

"But no horse could ever cross that?"

"These mountain ponies can. Still, the men usually get off and lead them. There's no necessity for taking unusual risks."

The warmth of the sun felt good after the forest chill.

"Now we turn up the mountain again," said her guide.

As they turned upward, Jane noticed again signs similiar to those she had seen posted in all conspicuous places along the trail. She had glanced at them rather carelessly, her thoughts dwelling on the beauty and novelty of the ride; but with the growing acquaintance with the forest, enveloped in its depths, and startled by some of Burnham's words, the signs assumed a new and ominous meaning. She paused to read:

[77]

Form 005.

FOREST FIRES!

The great annual destruction of forests by fire is an injury to all persons and industries. The welfare of every community is dependent upon a cheap and plentiful supply of timber, and a forest cover is the most effective means of preventing floods and maintaining a regular flow of streams used for irrigation and other useful purposes.

To prevent forest fires Congress passed the law approved May 5, 1900, which—

Forbids setting fire to the woods, and

Forbids leaving any fires unextinguished.

This law, for offenses against which officers of the FOREST SERVICE can arrest without warrant, provides as maximum punishment—

A fine of $5,000, or imprisonment for two years, or both, if a fire is set maliciously, and

A fine of $1,000, or imprisonment for one year, or both, if fire results from carelessness.

It also provides that the money from such fines shall be paid to the school fund of the county in which the offense is committed.

THE EXERCISE OF CARE WITH SMALL FIRES IS THE BEST PREVENTIVE OF LARGE ONES. Therefore all persons are requested—

1. Not to build larger camp fires than are necessary.

2. Not to build fires in leaves, rotten wood, or other places where they are likely to spread.

3. In windy weather and in dangerous places, to dig holes or clear the ground to confine camp fires.

4. To extinguish all fires completely before leaving them, even for a short absence.

5. Not to build fires against large or hollow logs, where it is difficult to extinguish them.

6. Not to build fires to clear land without informing the nearest officer of the FOREST SERVICE, so that he may assist in controlling them.

This notice is posted for your benefit and the good of every resident of the region. You are requested to cooperate in preventing its removal or defacement, which acts are punishable by law.

JAMES WILSON,
Secretary of Agriculture

From this warning and appeal her eyes turned to another notice attached like its companion to a stately tree trunk.

[78]

REWARD

FOREST FIRES

UNITED STATES DEPARTMENT OF AGRICULTURE,
OFFICE OF THE SECRETARY,
September 23, 1910.

Hereafter, during the fiscal year ending June 30, 1911, unless otherwise ordered, and thereafter, provided Congress shall make the necessary appropriation or authorize the payment thereof, the Department of Agriculture will pay the following rewards:

First. Not exceeding $250, and not less than $50, for information leading to the arrest and conviction of any person, in any United States court, on the charge of willfully and maliciously setting on fire, or causing to be set on fire, any timber, underbrush, or grass upon the lands of the United States within a National Forest.

Second. Not exceeding $100, and not less than $25, for information leading to the arrest and conviction of any person, in any United States court, on the charge of building a fire on lands of the United States within a National Forest, in or near any forest timber or other inflammable material, and leaving said fire before the same has been totally extinguished.

Third. All officers and employees of the Department of Agriculture are barred from receiving reward for information leading to the arrest and conviction of any person or persons committing either of the above offenses.

Fourth. The Department of Agriculture reserves the right to refuse payment of any claim for reward when, in its opinion, there has been collusion or improper methods have been used to secure the arrest and conviction thereunder, and to allow only one reward where several persons have been convicted of the same offense or where one person has been convicted of several offenses, unless the circumstances entitle the claimant to a reward on each such conviction.

These rewards will be paid to the person or persons giving the information leading to such arrests and convictions upon presentation to the Department of Agriculture of satisfactory documentary evidence thereof, subject to the necessary appropriation, as aforesaid, or otherwise, as may be provided by law.

Applications for reward, made in pursuance of this notice, should be forwarded to the Forester, Washington, D. C.; but a claim will not be entertained unless presented within three months from the date of conviction of an offender.

In order that all claimants for reward may have an opportunity to present their claims within the prescribed limit, the Department will not take action for three months from date of conviction of an offender.

(Signed) **JAMES WILSON,**
Secretary of Agriculture.

"I want to show you a cabin in here," Burnham said. He left the trail and started in—

anywhere it seemed to her. Jane loosened the reins of her pony and let him follow. But Dempsey merely took advantage of her to nip the green leaves of the salal and the tender tips of the fern brakes, as well as to carry her so close to the tree trunks that she was almost scraped off —an old, old trick of Indian ponies. Burnham turned and caught the difficulty.

"Hold up your reins," he said, "and switch him."

Dempsey's reformation was slow, but repeated applications of the switch prevailed.

Burnham suddenly drew up his horse.

"There it is."

"What is?"

"The cabin I spoke of."

Jane looked for it. She could see nothing but the great firs and cedars around her—no clearing, no cabin, no sign of human habitation. Burnham laughed. "Don't you see it?"

"Indeed I do not."

"It's that stump there." He pointed with his whip. Jane's eyes followed the whip but she was as puzzled as ever. It was not until Burnham led the way close to the other side of the

stump that she saw that a sloping roof of bark
had been fastened to the top of an immense
empty stump.

"Do you mean that some one really lives
there? I think you are making game of me,"
she added, half offended.

"Indeed I am not. A squatter really used to
live in that stump. That is his house—or was.
I don't know where he is now."

Jane still doubted.

"I 'm telling you the gospel truth," insisted
Burnham. "It is not an impossible thing out
here. Did you never hear of the family over
near the Sound who came out with six children
and lived in two great stumps until the man
could build a cabin? They roofed it with split
cedar, cut small holes for windows, cleaned out
the charred inside, and actually lived there for
several months. I 've heard that his wife said
she liked it because the hollows in the burned-
out roots made such good "cubby holes" in
which to store things away. That 's historical,"
he added. "And after they built their cabin,
they used one of the stumps for a barn."

"I think I should prefer a cabin—with a

[81]

comfy rocking chair," Jane answered, with a sudden sense of weariness.

Burnham made no answer and turned back to the trail.

"How far are we from the claim?"

"About three miles. We're almost there."

It was nearer five.

He started off to tell her in his own cheery fashion tales of forest life. He talked brightly, one foot free from the stirrup, half turning so that she could hear him without effort. He told her of the life he knew—of men who worked in the sawmills, of encounters with cougars and brown bears, of hunting trips through the higher mountains outside of the reserve, and of camp fires under the open stars.

"This is the result of an avalanche."

They had come to the edge of the trees again and there lay before them a tangled mass which nothing but an avalanche could have occasioned. For a distance extending nearly an eighth of a mile, according to her gauge of distances, there was one fearful tangle of broken trees and branches, interlocked and interlaced, with great masses of earth and rocks pinning them down at

Material for a bonfire prepared by an avalanche

intervals. Large trees had been snapped off as though they were pipe stems and hurled down the mountain side like jackstraws. Dry twigs and smaller branches lay scattered over the trunks and in the interstices. Over all was a fresh growth of green bushes, gleaming and waving in the warmth of the September sun. The mountain side directly above was denuded of trees—a mass of bare rock.

Both riders slackened their bridles and the ponies stood with drooping heads so characteristic of them, while the new homesteader and her guide looked out over the wreckage. Then up the mountain side, around the top of the mass, they started, to come down again on the other side.

Jane's mind went back to forest fires.

"What a bonfire that would make!" she remarked, pausing a moment as they turned, looking down on the mass of dry, twisted, and torn trees.

"Heaven help us if it ever does get afire," said Burnham gravely. "But really, there is little danger. That has been here for years, just as it is now. With the forestry service we

[83]

have now, there's little danger. But *what* a bonfire it would make!"

On and on plodded the horses, just as they had done through all the morning. Jane was growing tired. The trees scratched her face, and she felt a sudden irritation at the constant need of brushing the branches aside from the trail. Suddenly Burnham stopped.

"At this point," he said, "the trail to your claim begins. Stop a bit and see if you can fix it in your mind. You wouldn't want to lose your way getting to your own cabin."

Jane looked about her. She could see no difference between this and a thousand other points on the long trail from Illahee. The trees were of the same general appearance, about the same size,—nothing was different.

"I can't see a distinguishing sign. I surely would get lost," she answered with a sudden sense of utter helplessness.

"See that blaze there." She had not. "I'll make it clearer." He sprang off his horse and with an ax made two distinct blazes on the north side and two on the west. "This is a corner, you see?"

The horses began to wind among the trees. Jane's sense of helplessness increased with every moment. It would take all her resourcefulness, she thought, and far greater powers of observation than she had yet developed to go out of sight of her cabin and not get lost.

"I'll blaze a distinct trail from that corner to your cabin," Burnham said, answering her unspoken thought. "But why did n't you stay in civilization where you belonged?" he added to himself. "You're not the type of woman to take up a claim in the forest."

He wondered, as he had wondered all day, why she was doing it. Fairfax had said she was a friend of his wife's and that was sufficient. And she certainly was an attractive girl. "Ought to be married, with some good man to take care of her," was his persistent masculine conclusion. He remembered he had come around to that every time. But why not? Women certainly were better off if happily married and in homes of their own. "And there's where she ought to be."

"Tell me something about Mrs. Patton," said Jane, conscious of the fact that he had suddenly

[85]

begun to study her rather than to amuse her with his cheery talk.

"She's a woman of about sixty, little, sharp-tongued, energetic as a steam engine, afraid of nothing, independent, and a good cook—a mighty good cook," he added appreciatively. Cooking must count, even in the forest.

"Why did she come out here?"

"Her son went to Alaska seven years ago and said he would come back when he made his pile. That's the last that's ever been heard of him. The daughter married and lives in Illahee. She lived with them, but did n't get along well with her son-in-law. They scrapped world without end, until one day he slapped her in the face, I believe. She was red hot and took up a claim."

"And she's my only neighbor?"

"Yes, except the squatter. Here we are."

CHAPTER V

BURNHAM'S CABIN

THE sound of men's voices and the tread of horses' feet broke the silence which had prevailed at Burnham's old cabin.

"Here we are again." The voice belonged to Goss, who alighted from Dick and let the bridle fall to the ground.

"At last!" answered Burnham. "Now for some supper and a bed." He picked up Bob's bridle and started to lead the horses away. A moment later Goss's voice hailed him.

"Wait a minute. Let me have the key."

"It isn't locked." Burnham started off again.

"Yes, it is."

Burnham fumbled in his pockets. There was no key there. He dropped the bridles and turned back to the cabin.

"The key is inside. I remember leaving it there Tuesday morning. The door was left unlocked for Ole. I brought some tools out for him." As he spoke he applied his hand to the door. It seemed to be fastened. Bracing his shoulder against it, the door gave an inch or two, showing but a line of dense black. "Push with me, Goss; this is strange." The two men braced themselves against the door. There was a crash inside and the door yielded suddenly several inches.

Goss squeezed through the narrow opening into the dark room. There was another crash, a fall, and Goss's voice.

"What in the *deuce!*"

The match he struck flickered and went out. Burnham followed him into the darkness.

Another match was struck. Another crash. In the glimmering light the cabin seemed to be filled with bales, boxes, and barrels. Burnham reached for a candlestick on the shelf near the door, and the next moment the steady gleam of the candle penetrated the room. A scene of wreckage met the eyes of both men.

"Looks like a freight yard!" said Goss cheerfully. He leaned on a case of tinned tomatoes and rubbed his shin.

"By Jove!" Burnham looked helplessly around him. Then his eye caught sight of the name on a bundle wrapped in burlap. "I told that idiot—" But words were of no avail.

In the center of the cabin floor—indeed filling the whole cabin—lay a heap of freight. A fireless cooker poised on top of several tottering cases threatened immediate descent. One end of a sanitary couch rested on Burnham's cook stove. A box marked "Glass. Handle with care" had in falling knocked out one of the stove legs and even the pipe was awry. Goss struck against the rocker of a large chair and a box of books landed on his foot. A box of breakfast food, meditatively balancing on top of the heap, decided in favor of lower elevation.

"It looks"—Burnham dodged the breakfast food in its descent—"as if some one had made a mistake." He spoke in a calm, diplomatic way. The fireless cooker lost its balance and dashed toward him. Burnham tactfully stepped aside, and then, with equal tact and self-possession, sat down on it. A little thing might make him lose his temper, but a calamity like this made him resigned.

The cabin was a discouraging sight to two weary men. Goss had been out on a two weeks' trip through his district, straightening out quarrels between the sheep men in the high meadow lands of the mountains, looking after and supervising the making of trails, fighting small fires which sprang up here and there as though by magic, and all in a dense forest with bridgeless streams and dangerous cliffs. Burnham had just come in after a three days' cruise through almost impenetrable underbrush.

"This is a jolly row." His tone was disgust itself.

Goss looked for an explanation but got none.

Neither man was in any mood to straighten out a freight yard that night, but something had to be done if they wanted supper and bed in the cabin. It was only an ordinary homesteader's cabin, a twelve-by-fourteen-foot affair, with two bunks at one end.

Burnham started for the sanitary couch, the clumsiest thing except the rocker, and set it off to one side. The box of china and glassware came out from under the stove and the leg was replaced while Goss tried to straighten the pipe. A match started the fire in the small stove, another started a blaze in the fireplace, and the prospect speedily became more cheerful. It did not take very long, after they had once started, to carry the lighter boxes and cases outside the cabin and dump them down beside the doorway. Yet both were irritated.

"I 'll get supper," volunteered Burnham, pulling out the hinged board which served as a kitchen table, and beginning to get out supplies of bacon and eggs. "Just throw things anyway." Both were ignoring the whinnying of the horses from outside. A ranger's horse gets better care than he gives himself, but a few minutes' waiting was not injuring them to-night. Burnham lifted an egg to crack it. He was not a nervous man, but when Goss set a box in the bottom of the big chair and then tripped again over the long rockers which flew up unexpectedly, while a rolled-up rug fell over and hit him in the face, Burnham dropped the egg on the floor. And then a sudden sense of the ludicrous struck the two, tired as they were.

Goss sat down on the rug and laughed until the tears came. Burnham dropped the bacon and knocked off another egg.

"What is it? *Who* is it? Matrimony, Jack?"

"Not by a darn sight. It's that pig-headed Swede."

"Complimenting the Swede does n't enlighten *me*."

But there was no answer.

Goss kicked aside boxes in a way which would have shattered any woman's ideal of men as protectors—of household goods, at least—and stepped out into the gloom to care for the horses.

Burnham, on the swinging table which hung against the wall, set out a miscellaneous array of ironstone china and tinware. The fire was crackling cheerfully and the fragrance of bacon, eggs, and coffee filled the room when Goss returned. A can of evaporated milk was produced from somewhere, with a loaf of bread, and the half famished men set down to their supper.

The meal over, Burnham piled up the dishes

roughly and set them on the broad board. The table, to use a quaint old phrase of his grandmother's, had been "skinned."

"Whose junk is this, anyway?" asked Goss as they dropped down before the fireplace each with his head in a cloud of blue smoke.

"Woman coming up to take a homestead."

"But this is all reserve."

"She's taken the relinquishment on Mullaney's claim."

"Next to the Widdy's?"

"Yes. Hansen was coming out to build her cabin and I told the freight agent to send the goods to where Ole was going to build the cabin. And here's where he lands 'em." He looked disgustedly at the cluttered-up cabin. "What's more, I told Ole to take the freight across the stream from the Widdy's where he was to build the house."

"So he brought them out here because he's going to build you a barn. But," he added a moment later, "what have you got to do about it?"

"I had word from Fairfax about it."

"When did she come?"

"About three days ago."

Goss turned and looked at the boxes, " 'Jane G. Myers,' " he read a moment later. "Does that stand for Jane Gemima? Humph! Well, Jane, your goods are not in the right place. But I 'd rather have your goods than you."

"Why?" asked Burnham with a sudden twinkle in his eye.

"I 've no friendship for *Janes,*" was the unexpected answer. "I can see her—I can see her! Tall?"

"Rather."

"Angular, lanky, awkward, raw-boned, sharp-voiced, straight hair drawn straight back —so tight she can't get her eyes shut—and twisted into a little hard knot at the back of her head." Burnham looked attentively at the spilled eggs on the floor—in the opposite direction from Goss. "Great familiarity with a cook stove," Goss went on, "or with a washboard, but little with social amenities. I never knew a *Jane* yet that did n't answer that description. I 'll bet I 'm right on this one."

The Old Nick himself was dancing in Burnham's black eyes.

"I think perhaps you 're right about the cook stove," he answered a little ambiguously.

"I know I am. Age, forty!"

"Ahem! Still, it might mean an occasional square meal for us when the Widdy 's in town." The Widdy was their one defense against the rigors of camp cooking, and the tasteless cuisine of the ranger's headquarters or the hotel at Illahee.

Burnham began to wipe up the spilled eggs. Goss rose and knocked his pipe against the chimney. "We wish you no ill luck, Jane," he remarked as he refilled and relighted it, "but you *may* wish that you had stuck to the wash-board, for homesteading in the forest is no joke."

Goss turned at a slight sound which might have been a chuckle, but Burnham, with a face as long as the moral law, was wiping up the eggs on the floor. What was the use of saying she had wavy hair and violet eyes? Sometimes it was better not to tell everything you knew. Anyway, that was what he had learned as a freshman.

"What possesses *any* woman to take up a

homestead?" asked Goss, his face wreathed in blue smoke from his short pipe as he turned back toward the supper table; "what possesses any woman to take up a claim, especially in a dense forest like this?"

"Value of the timber, I suppose."

"But the hardships."

"I don't suppose it is any harder, come right down to it, than a washboard or a cook stove. And probably there's more money in it."

Burnham relighted his pipe and dropped down into his chair. Goss wandered over to the side of the cabin.

"Sanitary couch," he announced, "fireless cooker, crex rug, *and* a good big rocker. Jane's up to date anyway." He pulled the rocker over toward the fireplace, shoving the rough camp furniture out of the way, and dropped down into it.

"It's comfortable—thoroughly so. I might visit Jane once in a while—when the Widdy is in town and we need a square meal, I mean. Only that type of woman actually hurts my eyes."

"You might turn your back on her and

smoke." Burnham kept his face turned well away from his friend.

"Do you suppose that a *Jane* could be disappointed in love and take to the forest as a refuge?"

"You're disposed to be witty—as well as speculative. Remember what your family think of your being out in the forest."

"They think I'm daft—but I know better. Did you locate the timber you wanted?"

"Not entirely. Surveying seems to be crooked somewhere. Have a hard trip?"

"Usual thing. Small fires which seem to start from spontaneous combustion. Those two sheep herders, though," he added more energetically, "have got to stop their fighting or I'll shoot one of them. I surely will."

"Think they are responsible for any of the fires?"

"Can't prove it. I have my suspicions, though."

"Charlie Howe was at Illahee ten days ago," remarked Burnham after a long silence. "Asked about you. I gave him a long spiel for his paper."

[97]

"What's he on now?"

"'Frisco *Chronicle*. Came up to write up the lumber industry of Washington. Said the fellows around 'Frisco had a big reunion last month."

"None of the foresters there, of course,—at this time of year."

"Dick Crite was. He went up to Alaska cruising, started prospecting, and came down with quite a pile."

So the talk drifted on about this man and that —men who were cruising the forests all along the Pacific coast, men with whom they had tramped and camped in the forestry school, some of whom had failed and some of whom were on the high road to success.

The cabin was blue with smoke when Goss pulled himself together with a sigh. A bed would feel good after sleeping on the ground. Burnham rose and cast a comprehensive eye over the unwashed dishes.

"There's enough clean ones for breakfast," he announced, man-fashion.

CHAPTER VI

GETTING SETTLED

FRIDAY.

Dear Hope:

At last I am here, after those four dreadful days in that dreadful little sawmill town. Mr. Burnham came with me and everything went smoothly, but I was excited after we turned up the Thunder Creek trail which leads, part of the way, almost alongside of a mountain torrent, from the main trail to my cabin. There is n't much trail about it, though; nothing but blazes on the trees and bushes that scratch your face. At last we came in sight of the cabins, and there was mine, half finished. It 's lovely. It is close beside the most beautiful mountain stream I ever saw. On the other side is Mrs. Patton's cabin. My cabin is set right in among the trees, though they are not so dense as farther back. The only clearing is that made by cutting down the trees so they could use the logs for building.

And it's *my* homestead! I feel so joyful. Next to the cabin is a magnificent fir that towers far up into the sky, beautiful and strong and straight. It is a perfect tree. They said they did not cut it for the cabin because the bole was too large. Imagine cutting that tree down! The cabin is so artistic, nestling down under this one big tree.

We had to go across a narrow tree bridge to see my new neighbor, and I don't like her—at first sight, anyway. She has the snappiest eyes I ever saw and a snappy way of jerking out words between her teeth that is almost fearsome. She stood in her cabin door and looked me over, and said, "Huh!" When Mr. Burnham introduced us, she looked at me again, and then at him—those snappy, gimlet eyes,—before she even acknowledged the introduction. She is to take me in until my cabin is finished and it's a good deal better than being in Illahee. I can spend my time watching the men finish my cabin.

We three had dinner together and then Mr. Burnham went on up the valley. He told me he had a log cabin which he built before this was in the reserve and he still uses it, as well as this Mr. Goss, as a sort of wayside station—no, I mean, a half-way house. It is close to the point where three trails branch and it is so convenient for the rangers as well as for him that they keep up the "establishment." He laughed when he called it that. I almost wish I were going with him. I suppose it is because I know he is a friend of Bert Fairfax's that I feel now as if he were the one friend I had in the world.

I spent the afternoon sitting on a log outside Mrs. Patton's door, watching the men work and the stream rush past. I don't wonder they call it Thunder Creek. It does make such a noise, and it must be deep, too. When the men stopped work for the evening I went over and explored my new house. The fresh-hewn wood is so fragrant. The cabin is tiny, just the usual twelve by fourteen feet. They are putting in only one window and the door. I had said especially that I wanted two windows, and I ordered them larger than they are. I also wanted broad eaves and there are no eaves at all. I thought that perhaps even in a log cabin I

might build something that would express in-
dividuality, but there's absolutely no difference
between my cabin and that of the roughest class
of homesteaders. They have built the traditional cabin and it's rather disappointing.

Mr. Burnham told me before he went away
that I ought to have the fir—he says it's a
Douglas fir—cut. I was simply shocked. It
would destroy every bit of the artistic setting of
the cabin. I thought he had better taste, but I
just told him I wanted it for a flag pole. He
might not have understood the artistic side of
it.

That first night Mrs. Patton offered me a bed
on the floor in her cabin, or blankets for sleeping out of doors. What *do* you suppose she was
thinking of? To sleep out of doors, in an unknown forest, with bears around, perhaps! But
I did n't want to sleep in her cabin if I could
help it. Finally I told her I would take the
blankets and go over and sleep on the floor of
my own cabin,—that I thought I could cover
the windows and block the door in case a bear
did come around, and she actually let me do it.

Me! My first night in the forest! I was scared stiff, but I would n't show it. I did n't expect to sleep at all, but I hardly remember putting my head down. I wonder where in the world my furniture is, anyway. Mr. Burnham said it had been sent out several days before but it is n't here. He must have been mistaken. If I had my own furniture I could have set the couch in the cabin, because sleeping on the floor is n't all it 's cracked up to be.

I do not see how I am going to make many improvements on my homestead around my cabin. I guess I will have to confine them to the open land on the back of the claim. The forest is very dense. The trees are so large and so wonderfully high, clear of branches half way to heaven, and the ground the most impossible tangle of fallen trees, vines, fern brake, under-brush—utterly impassable. Is that a pun? I did n't see it until after it was written. The animal life, they tell me, consists of rabbits, squirrels, deer, bears, cougars, wolves, and wood rats, ranking in importance as named. I believe I 'm most afraid of a bear.

MONDAY MORNING.

The carpenter asked me this morning what that big roll of wire screening was for, so I showed him how I wanted a little extension on the end of the cabin, with a second, smaller door into it. He objected and refused until you would have thought it was his house and not mine. At last I appealed to Mrs. Patton. She came over the bridge—I found out afterwards how she dreaded that bridge—and listened to both of us, and said "Huh" again. But the Swede is so stupid! I explained what I wanted, —a place for my kindling wood in winter—and they both looked as if I had gone crazy. I insisted and at last I got the extension built—just two uprights at the proper distance from the cabin, with two boards around the bottom, a roof of shakes, and the rest of the wire screening. Then he had to cut a small door into the "pen" as he called it, but he certainly made it small and low enough. I can't see why they objected. They are putting the shakes on the roof to-day. To-morrow I can begin to move in.

Yesterday Mr. Burnham came up. I was so glad to see him. Sunday is rather lonesome in a strange place, and he took away the homesickness that was beginning to swallow me up. He is full of fun and life. He told me that I would not realize for a year what a tenderfoot I was. I fancy there are interesting experiences ahead, but I really don't care what they are. I 'm just in the mood for homesteading to-day and the more exciting the adventures, the better. I hope lots of things will happen.

Mr. Burnham spoke about cutting that Douglas fir again. I told him decidedly I would not hear of it. He argued a little while and then we dropped the subject.

TUESDAY.

The mail here is an uncertain thing, so my letter is taking the form of a diary. Please don't criticise the English or the continuity of it. I am just jumbling things up as they come.

My furniture came this morning and I am still wondering where it has been all this time. I spoke to Mr. Burnham about it Sunday, but he did n't seem to know much about it. The minute it came, I began to unpack. I got the couch in, first of all, and then unrolled my blankets, so my bed's ready for me to-night anyway. There will be some delay about the second window because they have to send to Illahee for the second sash, but they have to build a barn out here somewhere, so they will do that later as they are on their way in again. I have put some screening over it temporarily. They tell me the wood rats get in everywhere. I believe I can use that screened part as an outdoor sleeping place in summer, but you should have seen Mrs. Patton's face when I told her that.

The crossbeams of my cabin are studded thick with hooks of all kinds, for with such a small room I must hang supplies above. A piece of bacon hangs on one hook, ham on another, salt, potatoes, a jug of vinegar, and another of molasses,—each on its own hook. My eggs I put in brine in a big crock. On a shelf, close up to the roof, I put my canned goods and soap, cornstarch, baking powder, cereals, spices, and such things. You see, I have to stock up for months and months ahead because sometimes the trail to the town is rather difficult in winter, I believe. It would be fun to walk in on snowshoes, I should think. I believe I'll try it some time when I need exercise.

They built in a big fireplace at one end, and that I shall use for my sitting room. At the other end is my kitchen with the little air-tight wood stove, flat topped, for cooking. I had to run the pipe the entire length of the cabin and use the big chimney. They could just as well have made two chimneys. There are stones enough in the creek, goodness knows. I shall have some fun this fall making furniture out of the packing cases. I didn't bring much with me—rugs, rockers, a good couch, and so on, enough to be comfortable. I have not forgotten I am to stay here for five years—unless I should decide to commute.

I saw enough of Mrs. Patton—they call her "the Widdy"—in taking my meals with her, to pause with astonishment. She is a thoroughly good cook. No wonder these rangers plan their trips so as to stop here for meals. But she is the most superstitious person on salt that I ever met. It is her universal remedy for evil or accident. The first time I started out on an

exploring tour—I did n't go two hundred feet
—she scattered salt on the ground behind me so
I would not lose my way. The first time I
crossed the bridge to my own cabin, she flirted
ahead—that 's the correct word, she is so small
and wiry,—she flirted ahead of me and scattered
salt on the bridge, so there would be no accident.
She occasionally puts salt on the pony's back to
keep his mane and tail free from burrs—put
there by evil spirits, I suppose. And after my
cabin was finished, before I could move anything in, she scattered salt on my threshold.
She still says "Huh," but I like her better than
I did at first. She really means to be kind, I
think. She simply had no idea of what it
would mean to me to sleep out of doors my first
night here. She did n't dream how I felt about
it. We will never be very congenial, but I
think we 'll get along together all right.

She has a married daughter living in Illahee.
There are three grandchildren, Sam, who sometimes visits her, and two smaller ones. Of her
son-in-law, Pat, she said little, but that was expressive. Yes, quite expressive.

There is some chance of mail going down in

the next day or two, so I am going to seal this letter. Anything else that happens will have to be waited for. But I'm thoroughly glad I have undertaken this venture. I'm going to enjoy every moment of it. I have written Sue and Bert Fairfax, of course, but I have told them only the sunny side of things. You know how they felt about my coming.

Your friend,
JANE.

P. S. I always leave the most interesting things for the postcript. That's to make sure that you read my letters all through. I forgot to tell you about the cloth label—no, it is n't exactly that—perhaps I might say sign. Oh, no! It's a *notice,* that's what it is, that is tacked up on my front logs. It is n't on the door, and I can hardly say my front wall. Anyway, this interesting sign says that Jane G. Myers has taken up as a homestead the northwest quarter of section 47,—I think it is—of township—I've forgotten the number. I'll have to memorize the thing in order to know where I live—and range so-and-so. It's a unique sign—to me. Perhaps I'll get used to it. The Widdy has proved up on her claim, but she leaves the faded cloth notice there—to save herself trouble, she says.   But it's a *very* interesting label.   I know now just where I live!

CHAPTER VII

✤ THE BERRY PATCH

"HELLO," said Jane cheerfully a morning or two later as she stepped out of her cabin and found a small boy surveying the primitive tree bridge which spanned the creek. She stepped carefully down upon the stones, dipped her bucket into the rushing stream and stepped back upon the earth.

"Who are you?" she asked as the visitor made no reply.

"Sam," was the brief answer.

"Sam who?"

"Sam," was the laconic reply.

"Samson, eh?" Jane looked at the bare-legged boy, hands deep in pockets, blue eyes, and red hair a tangled thatch.

"You belong to the Widdy?" she asked.

"Yep."

"When did you come?" Jane felt really sociable. Her days as school teacher were not so

[111]

far past, though then it seemed ages since she had tried to teach just such boys as Sam.

"Last night."

"Walk out?"

"Nope."

"Sam, you will be a millionaire. They always begin that way—and they begin young."

Sam stared at her, open-mouthed.

"Good morning," said a pleasant voice behind her. The rush of Thunder Creek had drowned the sound of Burnham's approach over the bridge.

"Good morning, Mr. Burnham. I was interested in our visitor. I believe he is an incipient millionaire."

"He might be an incipient imp—with that head of hair," responded Burnham as he picked up the pail of water and started for Jane's cabin.

Sam suddenly turned and made for the bridge. Burnham glanced in that direction and saw the Widdy making motions.

"Breakfast must be ready," he explained as he set the pail down at the door and prepared to follow Sam. "By the way, I brought up two letters and a paper for you last night—and a package."

"I 'll come right over and get them," answered Jane. "No one came out last week and no one went in, so I have n't had any mail since I came."

In the roar of the creek the last words were lost, but the mill owner had little difficulty in guessing their import.

It was a delightful September morning. The fresh air, with the cool tang of the Northwest, the sunshine glorifying the clearing, the musical thunder of the water, the fragrance of the early morning, all made Jane Myers well satisfied with her change from city schools to the open life of the forests. She glanced back at her cabin as she neared the Widdy's door. It was really very picturesque backed by the dark, impenetrable forest and flanked by the foaming white stream.

Burnham glanced at her curiously. He had wondered many a time whether she regretted her venture, but she was the picture of contentment this morning as she greeted her neighbor cordially.

"I came over to get some letters Mr. Burnham said he brought out."

"All right," said the elder woman as she turned to Burnham, "Breakfuss' ready. You'd better come right in." Then she turned back to Jane: "I knew there'd be two people here 'fore night. I told Sam so."

Burnham lingered on the step, hoping that the Widdy would invite Jane to breakfast. Jane lingered a moment because she suddenly realized it was good to have some one to talk with.

"How did you know it, Mrs. Patton?" she asked.

" 'Cause I sneezed twice when I got up. It allus comes true. I told you so," she added a little suspiciously and Jane suddenly remembered she had heard of that omen before.

"Oh, yes, I remember." Silence fell. There was no invitation and Jane betook herself across the creek to her own cabin.

She had finished her own breakfast and was washing her dishes when she saw Burnham leading his horse across the stream.

"I came over to say good-by," he said in his usual cordial way. "I am going up into the for-

ests for a week or ten days. Perhaps I will see
you as I pass down again."

He had not had the slightest intention of adding that last remark, but something in her face
made him feel the sudden sense of loneliness
which had swept over her.

"I will be glad to see you when you come,"
she answered, her face brightening at the sense
of comradeship which lay behind the words.

"Are you lonely?"

He had not meant to ask that, either.

"No, really I am not—only sometimes."

"Yes, I understand."

He swung himself easily up on his horse and
sat there a moment looking down upon her.

"Don't get lonely—don't let yourself," he said
seriously. "The moment you do you will sink
under the horror of something which does n't
exist. You must remember that here in the
forest we are all good comrades."

And with a swing of his hat and a bright
smile, Jack Burnham vanished among the
trees.

"She's plucky," he said to Bob, as his four-
footed comrade picked his way sagaciously

down the trail. "If she can pull through the first winter, I believe she will stick it out."

But the world was suddenly very empty to Jane. The sun still shone, the light breeze waved the topmost branches of the pines and firs, but the rippling music of the trees was lost in the crash of waters. There was suddenly something ominous in the sound. It was no longer simply the dancing of the foaming waters, sheathed in white, in the September sunshine.

"Cheer up, Jane. This won't do."

The words brought back the memory of the day of the parody, the ruined hat and the burned drawn-work. How long ago it all was! It was ages ago, out in some other world, and it must have been some other Jane. She suddenly thought of Sam. The boy was fishing in the creek.

"Sam," she called as she went toward the child, "don't you want to go up to the clearing with me. There must be plenty of huckleberries there."

Sam stared.

"Don't you like huckleberry pie?"

A smile of joy and a nod of the tousled head.

"If you will come up to the clearing with me, I will make you a big pie, all for yourself."

Down went the fishing rod and Sam solemnly joined the homesteader.

"We'll get some pails and tell Mrs. Patton where we are going."

"Gran'ma?" asked the monosyllabic boy, hardly recognizing the Widdy's society name.

"Yes; we'll tell gran'ma we're going for berries and that I'll bake you a big pie when we get back."

There was nothing "sesquipedalian" about the Patton family. The Widdy was as monosyllabic as Sam when Jane told her of the berrying trip.

"Huh. Bears," she snapped.

There was reason for the snappiness. The horseshoe over the door had dropped.

"Oh!" Jane had not been in the forest long enough to think far ahead. "They won't want to eat me," she said hopefully after a moment's thought, remembering there was little danger from ordinary bears in berry time, "they'll be eating the berries. And I'll take my gun."

Bears or no bears, she felt she had to get out

into the clear sunshine that day. The dimness of the forest was depressing with the world so suddenly empty.

Up through the woods they trudged, by a trail which the Widdy pointed out, to a berry patch at the edge of the open land on her own homestead. It was not far away in reality, but through the forest tangle it took a long time. There was no actual trail. They merely took the line of least resistance. The heavy, glossy leaves and branches of the salal bushes with their tangle of tough roots seemed ever in their way. An occasional jump from bare-footed Sam revealed the presence of the prickly leaves of the Oregon grape, just turning, in the sunshine, to a glowing crimson. The treetops met overhead and the light which filtered through was cool green. Moss-covered trees lay in their path, covered with fern brake as tall as she, with long swordlike ferns, and with more salal.

"This *is* a tangle," said Jane as they came to one spot. She had followed a tree trunk which seemed to offer its services as a bridge across a maze of fallen trees—trees which had evidently fallen years before. "What if we should lose our way, Sam?"

There was no response.

"Do you suppose we can get through here, Sam?" She spoke rather anxiously. "I don't believe—I *know*—" She paused abruptly.

Still no response.

"Sam, I'm afraid—Good heavens! *Sam!*" For Sam had vanished. With her heart in her mouth, Jane looked about her. It was still the tangle of decaying tree trunks, covered with dense underbrush, and the tall straight growth of trees in their prime. *What* had become of the boy? He had been there a few moments before.

Again and again Jane's frightened voice rang through the trees. There was no answer from Sam or from anything else. What else she expected to answer her, she did not reason out. At last, as the thoroughly alarmed girl stared about her, there was a slight motion in the ferns and bushes some thirty feet away. Walking in that direction, Jane was amazed to see Sam's red head coming cautiously up through the space between two fallen tree trunks.

"Where in the world, Sam—"

"Fell in," responded the boy with more energy than he had yet shown.

"Fell in where?"

"Down there," motioning with his bare foot to an indefinite space beneath the trunk on which they were standing.

"How could you? Is there a hole down there?"

"You bet."

"A big one?"

"Yep. Betcher."

"How big?"

"Awful big."

Jane looked at him incredulously. How big was *big* to a red-headed boy? Still, the boy had dropped completely out of sight for several minutes—unless he was playing some joke on her. She looked at him searchingly.

"Can you get that for me?" Jane pointed to a pole some twenty-five feet long—a sapling which had been crushed and half-broken off. Sam obediently pulled and tugged at the dead sapling until he had wrenched it loose.

"You carry these pails until I see how deep

that hole is. Be careful. Don't fall in there again."

Jane lifted the pole upright, jammed the end of it through a space near that through which Sam had wriggled out and lowered it. Down it went, ten feet—fifteen feet—twenty feet, until to her amazement, as the pole touched something which impeded its further progress, less than two feet remained above ground.

"What is it?" she asked the boy. "Have these trees fallen across an old ravine?" That seemed the only solution.

"You betcher," was the emphatic reply.

"Are you sure? Have you ever seen a ravine covered over this way before?"

"Yep, lot of times. The trees is so big."

Sam's fright seemed to have given him unusual powers of speech. Bears lived in such sheltered places, he told Jane, and she gripped her gun more closely. But by the time Sam got through talking they were out in the open sunshine at the edge of the meadow.

The excitement of the hidden ravine, the clear sunshine, the abundance of huckleberries, big bunches of spicy, purple Oregon grapes, and the interest of the boy, put out of Jane's mind the sense of loneliness. The old spirit of adventure came back. They filled the pails and sat down to rest.

Sam was still fairly loquacious. His first demand was for a story. A story! Jane's mind went back rapidly over those she had told her pupils in school. None seemed to fit the occasion.

"A story about what, Sam?"

" 'Bout Injuns."

"Indians?"

"Yep."

Jane tried to think of a good Indian story. Suddenly she remembered a tradition Burnham had told her on their journey out.

"All right, Sam. Now sit still." Then she began an Indian tradition of the first white man's ship ever seen.

"Long, long ago, before white men knew anything about this Northwest Coast, a strange thing happened to some Indians who lived on the seashore near the mouth of the Columbia river, and this is the way the Indians tell the story.

"The son of a woman had died. She wailed for him a whole year and then stopped. Now one day she went to Ne Ahk-stow (near Seaside), and returned home walking along the beach. When she came near the Indian village at Clatsop, she saw something. She thought it was a whale. When she came nearer, she saw two spruce trees standing upright in it. She thought, 'Behold! It is no whale. It is a monster.'

"She reached the Thing and saw that the outside was all covered with bright metal. It was copper, but she did not know it. Ropes were tied on those spruce trees and the Thing was full of iron. Then a bear came out of it. He stood on this Thing that lay on the beach. He looked like a bear, with long hair, but his face was like a man's.

"Then the woman went home, but as she thought of her son she wailed, 'Oh, my son is dead and the Thing we hear about in tales is lying on the beach.' She thought this strange Thing on the beach and the bear were from the ghost land. So she kept on wailing.

"Now the Indians in the village heard her

wailing. They said, 'Oh, a person comes crying! Perhaps some one has struck her.' So they got out their bows and arrows and made ready to fight. But the Indian woman kept crying, 'Oh, my son is dead and the Thing we hear about in tales is lying on the beach.' Then the Indians began to run down the shore toward the Thing. The woman told some of them, 'A Thing lies on the beach. There are two bears in it,—or maybe they are people.'

"Now when the Indians reached the Thing that lay on the shore, two bears stood in it and they had copper kettles in their hands. Then the Indians saw that the Thing was really a great 'canoe' with two trees standing in it. It was a very strange-looking canoe. Then they began to watch the bears.

"The bears built a small fire, put some corn in a kettle, and soon it began to pop. The Indians were so surprised to see that corn fly up and down as it popped! Then the bears made motions to show that they were thirsty. So the chief sent two Indians to get fresh water while he went on the ship to look at the bears. They looked like men. He compared their hands with his. They were just alike. So were their faces alike, only the strangers had long beards and that is why the Indians thought they were bears.

"After a while, one of the Indians went down into the hold of the ship. It was full of boxes and he saw long strings of buttons there. He went to call his relatives, but before he could get back, other Indians had set the ship on fire. They wanted the metal in it.

"So these two men were prisoners and their ship was burned.

"Now all the Indians for a long distance around heard of this strange canoe with the two strange men in it. Whole tribes came down to Clatsop to see them and each tribe was anxious to get one of the 'bears' for a slave. They almost went to war over them. At last the chief of the Clatsops took one man as a slave and the chief of the Willapa Indians, who lived farther north, took the other.

"The Clatsop Indians became very rich because they sold the metal from the ship. A piece of iron five or six inches long would buy one slave. A piece of copper as wide as two fingers and long enough to go around the arm for a bracelet was also the price of a slave. One nail was the price of a good deerskin. So the Clatsops became very rich.

"But whose ship was this? And who were the men? No one knows. No one even knows whether they were Japanese, Chinese, or Spaniards. The ship was wrecked on the beach and the men became the slaves of the Indians. They were, perhaps, the first white men to see this coast. But we know about it only because the Indians told the story. No one else could know."

Jane glanced up as she finished her story, and as if a miracle had happened, over the treetops in the distance she saw the tip of a snow-capped mountain, dazzling, gleaming, in the bright sunlight. It must have been hidden behind the cloud banks. The world was suddenly very bright. She was glad she had taken up a homestead,—glad she had come to the valley of the Illahee. Free, with her own cabin, living in the open, with good comrades to whom she could talk now and then as they passed on the trail—what more could she want?

"Look!" said Sam, pointing toward the snowy peak.

"Yes, I see. Is n't it beautiful, Sam!"

But Sam only nestled more closely to her, with his hand still outstretched. He was rather heavy and his weight was not altogether comfortable.

"Look!" he said again in a low voice.

"I am looking."

"Is 't a bar?"

"What? Where? Bear?"

"There!" Sam's finger still pointed toward the mountain—or under it to a clump of small spruce trees.

With a sudden fear Jane seized the gun at her side. She, too, had caught sight of something dark behind those spiky Christmas trees.

"Let 's go," said the boy.

His frightened voice startled Jane.

"All right. Let 's pick up our things and go—quick."

Sam promptly upset one of the berry pails, scraping back more grass and dead leaves than berries. Off they started hurriedly.

Jane looked back every now and then, fearing

what she might see. As she gained the edge of the trees and looked back, she saw something dark standing among those young spruces. It immediately dropped to earth again, but in that hurried, startled glance it looked like the figure of a man.

"Sam," she said when she could get her breath, "take these pails and carry them carefully. Don't fall into any more ravines. And I'll carry my gun so that I can shoot if I see—er—a bear."

Sam stolidly carried the pails, walking carefully with simian skill along the tree trunks when they came to the old covered ravine. Jane was no less careful, for she had no desire to visit the lair of any wild animal. But she did some busy thinking.

If a man, who could he be? Surely not a forester or any man who had a right to be in the forest. An outlaw? But it must have been a bear. They look like men when standing up-right, especially with a screen of young spruce trees between. Yet a bear would have been among the berry bushes, not spying on her from the shelter of the young spruces. And down in her heart she was sure that the creature had two feet and two hands, not four feet.

"Yer back early," said the Widdy as the two came up to her cabin door.

"Berries were plentiful and it did n't take long. It was beautiful. A glorious snow peak was in view. We had some adventures, too. Sam fell into an old ravine covered by fallen trees, and we saw a bear."

"Nope," said Sam firmly, "a man."

"A man?" shrilled the Widdy.

"Yep."

"One of them forest men?" She looked at Jane suspiciously.

"No, indeed. I don't know whether it was a bear or a man. It was *something* watching us from behind some young spruce saplings. We did n't wait to see. I got my gun and gave Sam the pails and we came back."

Her rather frightened voice betrayed her.

"I knowed it," said the Widdy ominously. "I knowed it." Jane remembered the fallen horseshoe.

"But nothing did happen, you see," she said regaining her quiet tone. "Nothing at all."

CHAPTER VIII

DOUGHNUTS

IT was only two days later that Burnham, riding his horse to his cabin one evening, saw smoke pouring from the chimney. A light from the open door brightened the gathering dimness of the forest.

A figure, black against the lamplight within, appeared at the door.

"Hello, Jack."

"Hello. Thought you were making trails up at the peak."

"I came down yesterday evening. The men are still up there."

Burnham dismounted and led his horse to the old shelter of poles and fir branches, stumbling over the new logs for the barn. There had long been a need for a barn there.

As he came into the house, fragrant with coffee and bacon, as usual, he found Goss cooking. The table was still hanging against the

wall with no dishes yet on it.   Burnham pulled
it out and tossed a few dishes upon it.   Then
Goss broke the silence.

"By the way, I had to interrupt your work on
the barn.   I found the bridge needed attention,
so I ordered the men down there.   We have all
we can do before winter is upon us."

"There's no special hurry about the barn.
They can do that any day."

"I sent them down several days ago.   They
ought to be back by to-morrow."

Supper over, there was the usual long silence
between them until the curling blue smoke of
their pipes had tinted the atmosphere.   Then
Goss spoke.

"Supplies are about out. Breakfast will
clean up everything."

"Everything?"

"Yes; bacon, ham, potatoes, coffee, sugar and
bread.   I thought there was plenty when I left
here."

"Grub thieves?"

"Looks so—unless the carpenters have helped
themselves.   I did n't care to question them."

"Who could it be?"

"I don't know, I'm sure. But everything is gone."

Burnham thought over the situation a few moments.

"I'll go down to the Widdy's to-morrow and see what she can spare. We bring her supplies up to her often enough."

It was nearly five o'clock the next afternoon when Jane, putting the last touches to her new cabin, saw Burnham come up the trail to the house. He stopped to pass the time of day and mention his errand.

"I am going to beg some supplies of the Widdy," he said in a pause in the talk. "It looks as though we had grub thieves up the trail. When Goss came back yesterday, nearly everything was gone."

Both glanced toward the closed door of the Widdy's cabin.

"Oh, I almost forgot," exclaimed Jane. "She went into Illahee this morning with Sam. But I can let you have supplies, and I should be very glad," she added, with more color in her face, "if you would take dinner with me. Besides, I should like to ask you about something."

[132]

"I shall accept with pleasure," was the prompt answer.

It was too late to get back in time for Goss's supper and the Swedes had returned to their barn building so he could borrow a few supplies of them.

It had been a matter of principle with Jane Myers that every woman should be a good cook, and though her last eight years had been spent in teaching and boarding where kitchen opportunities were scant, she had nevertheless made it a point not to forget the early lessons in cooking. Her mother had been a famous cook. That particular day, too, as it happened, Jane had been possessed of a sense of sudden forlornness when she saw Dempsey step down the trail with Mrs. Patton on his back while Sam trotted alongside. Dempsey knew well how to carry the two, but Sam preferred to walk for a while. The light seemed to go out for a moment when the bright red head vanished among the bushes. So Jane, haunted with the sense of an empty world, had spent the day putting finishing touches to her cabin, baking bread and ginger cakes, and planning an elaborate dinner for one.

But it was to be a dinner for two, as it turned out, and Burnham was glad enough to sit down to the table with its white cloth, china which was neither ironstone, nor tin, and a dinner of something beside bacon and eggs and potatoes. Hot rolls just out of the oven, jam, creamed eggs such as neither he nor the forest ranger could cook, asparagus tips, scalloped tomatoes, and more than that, a pleasant-faced girl with brown hair and violet eyes to pour out his coffee and talk to him. He blessed Bert Fairfax for his letter of introduction. Such good comradeship in so short a time would otherwise have been impossible, as he well knew, despite the exigencies of forest life.

Time flew quickly enough as they dropped down into comfortable chairs before the open fireplace. He stretched himself in the big rocker which had tripped up Goss. A sudden memory of it made him laugh. He sat up and looked down at the rug under his feet. The very one which had hit the forester in the face!

The joke was too good a one to keep. Jane's inquiring face brought out the whole story, and a good laugh they had over the freight yard in that other cabin, five miles up the trail.

"And your friend?" she asked. She wondered a little that she had not seen him.

"Did n't you see him when he was down?"

"No."

"That 's strange. He was down for dinner three days ago at the Widdy's—why, he 's been down here twice since you 've been here."

"I have n't seen him."

"You will. Goss is a splendid fellow, but I don't know just how sociable he is to women."

"Why is he out here?"

"He loves the forests—and—and— Why are you out here?"

He could n't resist the temptation, and she had given him too good a chance to ask that question.

"I have taught school for eight years and I was dead tired of it. A friend of mine took up a homestead in Colorado and she seemed to find it such fun, it influenced me. But I wanted the forests."

"The timber is worth more of course—if you sell it."

"It was not only that, but the open plains do not attract me. I care more for the forest."

"It is much more dangerous."

"Really?"

"Yes, in many ways."

"But there would be no real danger here for me!"

"I hope not." He answered in a rather non-committal tone. "What did Fairfax say about your coming?"

"He disapproved of it. Said it was no place for a woman, but that was because Sue was so shocked at the idea. Sue isn't the pioneer type, and Bert Fairfax isn't either. They thought I ought to stay in the city and teach until—" She hesitated with a little embarrassment. She had not intended to say so much.

"Until you get married? I hope you are not a man hater."

"No, indeed. But I think every woman has a right to plan her life as makes it happiest for herself."

"And you mean to say that you are happier out here, alone in the forest and in the midst of real danger, than with your friends in a city?"

"I was so tired of the routine of teaching. Besides, I only have to stay here five years, or if I wanted to I could commute in less time than that, could n't I?"

"You can commute, but I don't know how easy it would be to prove up on your claim if you abandon it the moment you get it. Several patents have been recalled on that score lately. It used to be possible, but the government is growing more rigid in its definition of homesteading."

"I could commute and stay here a year or two more, and then come here summers?"

"Perhaps. Yes, I guess so. But even then that's two or three years out here in the forests."

He caught sight of her mandolin. "Sing something for me," he asked.

Jane glanced at the clock.

"May I ask you something first? You mentioned danger and that reminded me of what I spoke of when you first came." She plunged into the matter head foremost and told him of the man in the berry patch.

Burnham's face grew serious.

"You are sure it was a man?"

"I was not so sure at the time. But Sam was positive, and the more I think of his appearance as I saw him just as we reached the edge of the clearing, the more certain I am it was a man. And then yesterday!"

"What?"

"Yesterday I went behind the cabin, just a little ways, following the creek up—"

"Alone?"

"Yes, but I had my revolver with me."

"Can you shoot?"

"Bert Fairfax made me learn last summer. I learned to shoot a little. But if I were frightened I am not sure that I could hit anything."

"I did n't mean to interrupt you. What did you see?"

"Nothing. That was just it. I heard a slight sound—or thought I did—and I turned in that direction just in time to see the bushes sway. I stopped short—and then I started over there —and then I stopped again. I thought when I stopped it might be a bear, or a cougar, or some animal, and then I heard that little sound again."

"You did n't see anything?"

"Nothing but the swaying of the bushes."

Burnham's face was grave. Should he tell her or not? What business did a woman have to come into such a place, anyway? Why should a good-looking teacher want to homestead in the wilderness? "There 's a love affair back of it somewhere," was his decision. For the moment he was inclined to tell himself that it was none of his business. She had been warned that there was danger. Fairfax had warned her, and he had. If he told his suspicions, she would be afraid to leave her cabin. If he did not, she might meet with some danger any minute. The Widdy was brave enough for herself, but the Widdy had had a hard life of it and gave little thought to generous actions for others. Even if she were more friendly, what good would she be if she were in Illahee, or even in her own cabin with that roaring creek between? No sound could reach her over the rush and thunder of those waters. And if the tree-bridge were ever removed, neither woman could possibly cross the stream. Then his sense of chivalry made him accept the responsibility.

He turned to find her studying his face.

"I know what you are thinking," she said. "You are wondering why I ever came here. Yet it's about as safe here, I fancy, as a city street—in any city. But if there is any danger, I want to know it. A hidden danger—the horror of something unknown—that is harder to face than any actual, acknowledged danger. What is it?"

"I think it must be the squatter."

"The tree-stump house man?"

"Yes. Did I tell you he was supposed to be a criminal of some sort in hiding—nobody knows what. He left here about two years ago and no one has seen him since. But he may have come back."

"But he's miles away."

"You mean the stump house is. He's likely to be anywhere. I fancy that's where our grub has gone."

"What shall I do?"

"Never go out of your cabin without your revolver or gun—and keep your revolver handy inside here, too. Practice shooting, every day, at long range. Never let your supply of ammunition or food get low. Are you well locked up here, when you are out, and at night?"

"Yes."

Burnham got up and examined the fastenings of the windows and door.

"They look strong. Moreover, get a good dog. You must have one. I am surprised that Fairfax did not see to that. And above all, Miss Myers, remember that here in this immense forest, we are all comrades. Never hesitate, from any sense of false delicacy, to ask anything of Goss or myself, or the Widdy either, no matter what it is, nor at what time. Will you promise that?"

"I should be putting too much responsibility upon both of you. And, besides, I have never met him—never even seen him, although you say he has been down here twice since I came."

"What difference does that make? He is a gentleman—out here in the forest to protect it because he loves it. Are n't you of as much value as a forest tree? I suppose he was in a rush when he was down here and ate his dinner and rode off."

"If you put it in that way—"

"I do put it in that way, most emphatically. Another thing is that we must ask you to follow our directions."

Jane hesitated. It was rather a broad request.

"We can't help you, you know, if you go off on a tangent just at a critical moment. And a man can never foresee just what a woman is going to do."

"I 'll promise this. I 'll follow your instructions when they seem at all reasonable." That was all the answer he could get.

Burnham glanced at his watch. It was later than he supposed—nine o'clock—and he had five miles to go. He glanced around again, gauging the safety of the cabin, nodded his head in approval, and started out for Bob. In a few moments he was back.

"Another thing, Miss Myers," he said to the girl standing in the doorway as he fastened the various food supplies to the saddle, with an especial pat on the sugar and coffee, "grub up the bushes around your cabin so that you have a clear view of things. It might not be a bad idea to get out the stumps as soon as you can have it done."

"Thank you, very much. I feel perfectly safe since I know I can at least talk things over with you. Good night."

"Good-night," he called back and half turned in his saddle, as Bob started down the trail, for a last view of the tall figure silhouetted against the light. As he passed into the blackness of the night, she turned and closed the door, giving first one shivery glance in the direction of the black, unlighted cabin across the creek.

It was nearly midnight when Burnham at last reached the cabin and his cheerful yodel aroused Goss, asleep before the fire.

"You're a slow one. What's happened? Did you bring the grub?"

"You bet. I did n't get over to the Widdy's until late."

"Have a good dinner?" Goss had had a very slim one.

"Yes." Burnham brought in the supplies as he spoke.

Goss looked them over. "Bacon, eggs, coffee, bread, sugar, potatoes—what's this?"

"Doughnuts. She had just baked 'em. Insisted that I should take them."

"Of course." There was silence for a moment as Goss opened the bag of doughnuts.

"H'm-m-m-m! Doughnuts! Where are the holes?"

Burnham turned around guiltily as Goss pulled out of a small sack a dozen small, fresh ginger cakes.

"I—I—er—ate the holes," he answered brazenly.

"Did the Widdy have company?" He could hardly imagine it, and though the figure of Jane Myers, gaunt, lanky, awkward and hard-handed, rose before his mind's eye, he immediately banished the picture. She would hardly interest him.

"No," answered Burnham.

"I suppose Jane is as tall and raw-boned as ever? I have missed seeing her when I was there."

"Jane is as tall as ever," answered Burnham cheerfully. "By the way, I have reason to think that the squatter is back in this section. I think that might identify our grub thief."

"Ole told me this afternoon that last week he saw a suspicious-looking man skulking around, just at dusk. Not one of them thought to watch him! But the description, such as I could get, seemed to fit."

Burnham looked serious. Then Jane was right. She had seen a man in the berry patch and it must have been the squatter. It was probably the squatter who had made the bushes sway. But there was nothing to be done. He had warned her of danger, and Fairfax had done so, and she would have to look out for herself.

Fifteen minutes later the heavy breathing of the two men from the bunks at the end of the cabin gave clear evidence that both Jane and the squatter were beyond the memory of either.

CHAPTER IX

THE DOUGLAS FIR

THE bridge was mended, the barn was finished and the carpenters were homeward bound. Supplies for Burnham and for the two homesteaders were coming out on the morrow on horses and the men would return on their backs. But the recollection of the Widdy's cooking prompted them to walk the five miles to the cabin and take the horses from there. Goss and Burnham were coming down as well, so the carpenters notified Mrs. Patton. And the Widdy was putting in a busy afternoon cooking. The money thus unexpectedly earned in the depths of the wilderness was of importance to her.

Burnham reached the cabins first and crossed the bridge to the Widdy's.

"Ole told you we were coming, did he? All right." Still he hesitated on the doorstep. Finally he turned back.

"Did you know that the squatter was back?"

"What squatter?"

"The man who used to live in the tree stump down the trail. He is supposed to be in hiding from the law—nobody knows. But it's well to keep your food locked up, and your revolver loaded, and not to leave your door unlocked. If you should get frightened, Goss or I—"

"If ye're not a hundred miles from here!"

"Of course. But we want to protect you and Miss Myers—any woman homesteader. By the way," and now Burnham was getting around to his point, "Miss Myers has never met Goss. I'd like it if you'd invite her over to supper with us this evening."

"Huh!" The Widdy could put an immense emphasis into a single word when she chose, but even more into a glance from her keen, shrewd eyes. "No, I'll not invite her. She'd better to stay whar she is. Huh!"

Burnham regained his dignity.

"This is a matter of importance. You may do as you please. I will see that she meets the forest ranger of this district. It's necessary so long as that squatter's around."

[147]

Silence was the Widdy's answer, and Burnham walked off across the bridge. But Fate had another sort of introduction in store for Jane.

Goss rode slowly up the trail and stopped long enough to take in with experienced eye the new cabin and its surroundings. He tied Dick to the nearest tree and strode down the trail a hundred feet to where the carpenters had camped. His colloquy with Ole Hansen was brief and apparently unsatisfactory. As he came up the trail again, Burnham crossed the bridge. Goss joined him.

"Jack, what does *that* mean?" he demanded. "I thought you were looking after this cabin business for her?"

"I was—I am—I know it." Burnham knew exactly what Goss's accusing forefinger meant. It pointed to the tall Douglas fir, six feet in diameter, a hundred and fifty feet high, towering into the blue sky.

"Are you crazy—or is she?"

"I urged having it cut—said everything I could. She would n't listen. Wants it for a flag pole."

"It *must* come down."

"Well, you see her then. Perhaps she will listen to you."

"Interview *Jane!*" Burnham's eyes twinkled at the tone. Evidently his companion had not yet seen her. "I will—for that tree is to come down."

Goss walked straight from the bridge to the door of the cabin. Jane, in her short skirt, was starting a fire in the cook stove. Goss tapped at the door.

"You are Miss Myers?"

"I am." Standing in the back of the cabin, with stove lid in hand, Jane saw merely a square-shouldered man at her door. She presumed it was Goss. But she had no wish to meet him and stayed where she was.

"Miss Myers, this tree will have to come down."

"What tree?"

"This fir near your cabin."

"May I ask why?"

"I don't consider it safe."

"You are Mr. Goss?"

"I am."

"May I ask if your authority extends to cutting down any trees you may wish?"

"In the forest I cut down any trees I consider dangerous."

"But this is my homestead."

"I am sorry. The tree will have to come down."

"Impossible." Jane's voice was firm enough. "I will not allow it to be cut down. It must remain where it is."

"Why?"

"Because it's beautiful—and it would be a protection in a storm."

"A deadly danger in a storm."

"It looks sound."

"It is sound. But it would blow over. You understand that all coniferous trees are very shallow rooted. This tree is peculiarly exposed because its immediate fellows are down. A high wind is likely to send that crashing into your cabin any day."

Jane had been gradually walking nearer the door, stove lid still in hand, while the fire in the cook stove flickered and blazed. Absent-mindedly she set the lid down on the floor near the door and stepped out to look at the tree in dispute.

"There are dangers everywhere," she said with great dignity, still looking at the tree. Then, with a sudden flash of humor, she added, "That tree is no more likely to fall down on my cabin than a cougar is to rip off my roof and drop in on me when I 'm not expecting any one to call."

"Well, that might happen, too."

Goss turned to Burnham.

"Jack, send those carpenters over here and tell them to cut this tree down."

Jane blazed. "You are impertinent, sir. This is my homestead and my cabin and my tree, and I will *not* have that tree cut down!"

She turned toward him for the first time. Goss squared his shoulders and walked over to where the angry girl stood. Drawing himself to his full height, he looked down into her face. It was actually the first time either of them had really looked at the other, and in each mind there was a distinct sense of surprise. "Goss is a king among men," Burnham had said, and Jane was suddenly conscious of his height, the breadth of his shoulders, the flush of health under the tan of the bronze face, but above all of a very commanding personality and a pair of keen gray eyes. Her own faltered under his steady gaze. He seemed to be looking right through her, searching her thoughts, and she suddenly felt like a three-year-old child. He, on his part, was suddenly aware of a trim figure, looking very slender and childish in the short skirt, a rather plain but pleasant face, crowned with wavy brown hair, and a pair of violet eyes where brown ones ought to be.

"I'll thrash Burnham," was his mental resolution, though it seemed to have no bearing whatever upon the tree question. Then he spoke, very kindly, but very firmly:

"Miss Myers, I am sorry. I understand your feeling for I love trees myself, but it *must* come down. It is too dangerous—far too dangerous."

It was the voice of authority, and there was no gainsaying him. The carpenters had come with their axes and saws, followed by Burnham who had taken in the whole situation. Jane turned and went into her cabin. Burnham, with the freedom of an old friend, followed her. He did not mean to startle her, but he would have sworn when she turned suddenly at his step that she wiped her eyes.

"Miss Myers, Mrs. Patton wants you to take dinner with us over there to-night."

"I am sorry, but I cannot."

"Miss Myers," he came over to her by the cook stove, "please do. Goss will be a good friend to you, even if he does seem unreasonable now. And he is really right about the tree. Besides, you can't refuse the Widdy without offending her, can you? And she is a pretty close neighbor, you know, in a place where neighbors are few."

"Yes, that is true."

"Then I will tell her you will come."

"Yes, I 'll come."

"I 'll come over for you."

He stepped outside the cabin again. Goss had given directions as to where the tree was to fall and the chips were flying as the men plied their axes.

"Hold up, Ole." Burnham, in a spirit of mischief, picked up Jane's camera which lay just inside the door. "I want a snap shot." The men stopped and faced him for a moment; then as he turned the roll, the chips began to fly again. Burnham quietly set the camera in a safe place outside the door and sauntered over the bridge.

"I invited Miss Myers to take dinner with us to-night—I will pay for it, of course,—and you will need to put another place on for her," he added as his eye scanned the table. "Mr. Goss also wants her here for dinner," and having thus diplomatically arranged things to suit himself, he sauntered over to Jane's cabin again.

"Poor girl," he meditated, as he watched the men drop their axes and pick up the long saw, "I'll bet she's madder than hops. The first scrap on earth between the first man and woman was over an apple tree. Suppose it had been a Douglas fir!"

When the saw became bound, wedges were slipped in to release it, and then back and forward it wove its way through the heart of the tree until, at a signal from Goss, they sprang back and with a crash which echoed through the forest the Douglas fir stretched its long length on the ground beside the trail.

The clang of a tin pan came across the ripple of the water. Dinner—or supper, as they called it,—was ready. Burnham approached Goss. "Miss Myers will take dinner with us to-night," he said. "The Widdy has invited her."

The air was soft and warm, and a bright light shone cheerfully from the cabin across the way, but Goss unconsciously pulled up his coat collar. Why in the world, of all nights, should the Widdy have invited Miss Myers to take dinner with her on this particular one? She would be angry, of course, at the fall of the tree. Goss rather dreaded that dinner table.

It was full ten o'clock that night before Goss and Burnham crept under their blankets, out in the open air, with a camp fire at their feet.

Since they had left the cabin Goss was no more silent than usual, but he was silent "in a different tone of voice," as Burnham would have expressed it.

Eerie shadows flickered in the dancing light

[155]

of the camp fire. Both lay watching the dancing gleams, making the ghostly trees advance
or retreat as a sudden blaze lighted up the somber trunks and the dark canopy so far overhead.

"What's the joke?" asked Goss, raising himself on his elbow as he heard for the tenth time
Burnham's familiar chuckle. Burnham chuc-
kled again.

"Did any man ever predict accurately what
a woman's going to do?"

"No; and never will."

With mutual impulse both men broke into a
peal of laughter.

"You ought to be ashamed of yourself, to lord
it over a helpless girl like that," said Burnham
finally.

"Ashamed! Ashamed! You use that word
to me, you imp, after deceiving me so about her."

"Never, never!" declared Burnham. "You
just made up your mind from the start what she
looked like—because her name was Jane—and
I let you fool yourself."

"Jack, if you ever play such a game on me
again—"

"I am innocent. It was all your own fault."
He laughed as he remembered Goss's face during that evening.

"It was high-handed, I admit, and I admired
her spunk—but that tree *had* to come down."

Again there was silence. One moment the
forest was black, the next, the trees, vague, huge,
dreadful, reflected the gleam of the fire.
Around them was the ripple of the water and
the strange night noises of the forest.

Burnham heard Goss chuckle.

"What is it?" he asked in his turn.

"Jack, I understood perfectly to-night why
you ate the holes in those doughnuts."

Again a peal of laughter startled the swaying
shadows.

"Well, now—"

"I learned the full extent of your perfidy
when I offered to pay the Widdy for the
borrowed grub. I'll thrash you well, next
time."

There was a moment's silence.

"She's game, all right," said Jack.

"She is," answered Goss briefly.

For Goss had been even more surprised than

Burnham over Jane's method of taking his high-handedness. He had been in the right and he knew it. Manlike, he respected her for yielding the point, "especially when she could n't help herself," he added. His logic, in true man-fashion, was not very clear when applied to women. He did not understand that she, womanlike, recognizing that he was in the right, respected him the more for his firmness. He probably never would know that his real conquest had come, not through his firmness or his determination, but through the kindness of the steady gray eyes. Had he won his point through harshness, she would have hated him. But a really strong man never needs to use harsh methods—with women, or men either.

So it was a surprise that Jane had come into supper that evening, not in her short khaki skirt, but in a long, graceful gown of some sort —he could n't remember what it was, only there was a touch of violet on it which just matched her eyes. And she had brought her mandolin with her, and had sung some old Scotch songs to them, and they had all sung together some old college songs. And Goss, as he watched her, had had an odd sense of surprise every time he saw those violet eyes—and above all a sense of amazement that such a girl as this could be named Jane.

So in the quiet of the forest they dropped asleep, Burnham to dream of falling stars with violet eyes that turned into Douglas firs which the carpenters persisted in hacking. Once a far-off crash in the forest aroused him enough to replenish the camp fire. But Goss slept the unbroken, dreamless sleep of the just.

CHAPTER X

IMPROVEMENTS

IF any one had ever told Jane Myers that she would join the ranks of people who constantly talk out loud to themselves, she would, in those days so long past, have hooted at the idea. It was with something of a shock that she found herself continually arguing with that Other Self, counseling with it, talking to it, after a month in her homestead, as though that Other Self were something quite distinct from her own self. Somewhere, back in civilization, she had heard that it was a sign of incipient insanity. But after thinking it over, she decided that the practice was really a sociable one, and that if she were only that much insane no one would find it out. "But if the Widdy catches me doing it, she 'll have a 'hunch,' or take it as a sign, or something," she told herself and her mental vision saw the Widdy's hand go for the salt box, the sure preventative against all evil.

Such streams as these vanish when the
forests burn

It was a glorious morning in early October, with the sun streaming down upon the creek which swirled and rippled along in quite a friendly fashion. The water was low, the Widdy had told her. Also that there were plenty of fish in the pond above. Jane had included a fish rod among her forest belongings.

But that morning, as she dipped a bucket of water from the creek, she decided to put on her gymnasium suit and begin grubbing up the bushes around the cabin. "A skirt is out of the question for that sort of work," she told herself impatiently. Improvements were required by law as well as safety, and Jane felt she might as well begin. It was too glorious to stay indoors.

She felt, as she came out of the door with her hatchet in her hand, that she was in the heart of romance. She could hear in the quiet the voice of the falls, some five or six hundred feet below, and the rush of the rapids above. Beginning at her very door was the long trail of the cathedral forest, and the morning air was fragrant with the faint forest spiciness. All around her was the immensity, the vastness, of

[161]

unexplored space, the mystery of the "hills of silence." There was a broad, shimmering light on the water of the creek now, revealing its restlessness and activity, calling her attention to it again and again from the mystery of the forest, but it was a very different place at night. With the glimmer of moonlight upon the white foam, with the broad patches of frosty white contrasting with the pitch blackness of the shadows, it was a spot where Oberon and Queen Mab might play, and where Puck surely came. Perhaps if she cleared the path to the creek she could see them.

"I wonder what all these things are, anyway," Jane looked about her as she spoke at the service berry bushes, salal, Oregon grape, sword fern, wild syringa, the great fern brakes almost as tall as she, the troublesome devil's club, and the nameless growth of the deep entangled forest. The trail to the water had broken down the frailer ones but the others remained as sturdy as ever. A great tree had once fallen across what was now that path, though the carpenters had cut it in two and pulled the lighter end away. But all around lay the decaying trunks of fallen trees, some apparently still sound, with sharp, spiney ends which caught in her clothing whenever she passed.

"It will take me five years to clear half an acre of this," she argued as she looked about her for a good place to begin. "But I am going to get some trails through."

Salal bushes went down under the vigorous strokes of the hatchet, and so did the clusters of Oregon grape. The crimson leaves she laid to one side for cabin decoration. Foot by foot in the cool October air the girl toiled, with the singing of the creek always in her ears.

"But it is positively wicked to cut down a bush like that," Jane insisted, as she came to the evergreen huckleberry whose dainty, glossy leaves had turned to a red bronze in the autumn nights. "Positively wicked." The shrub stood four feet high, its reddish leaves gleaming in the sunlight. "I shall regard the presence of that huckleberry bush as an improvement."

Jane glanced over at the line of smoke rising from the Widdy's cabin. "I wish she were more sociable. Wish she were a girl and would come out and play with me." The slight figure of the Widdy passing and repassing her cabin door was the only answer. "Wish the stream were not between us; then we could call back and forth to each other. But we can't do that over the music of the water." She grubbed for an hour more, then decided a change of work would be a rest.

"Jane, our next endeavor will be to cut some kindling wood. We have a good deal to cut before winter sets in." She glanced at the pile of odds and ends thrown together by the carpenters on top of some cord wood which they had split. "You have to provide three-foot wood for your fireplace and smaller bits for the cook stove."

When Burnham had suggested that a man should come out and cut her winter's supply of wood, Jane had demurred. "I am sure I can do it," she had insisted with all the certainty of a tenderfoot. "I want the exercise, you know."

Burnham's face had at first been blank, then amused. "Do it at once, then," he had said with decision,—"do it at once." And afterwards added. "Let me know when you want a man."

At noon Jane went in to cook her luncheon.

The fireless cooker had proved to be a joke. She had bought it thinking it would be a convenient way of doing her cooking when she wanted to be out of doors all day, in the sunshine. But the sight of it soon palled upon her. There was nothing homelike, nothing sympathetic, about it. No chance to stir the fire, no fragrance of burning wood, no gleam of a blaze through the lid, no watching the steaming pot while wondering if the vegetables were almost done, no dripping the gravy over a roast, none of the familiar fragrance of the cooking dinner. It was like taking her dinner out of a blank-looking tool chest.

So the fireless cooker, ignored and humiliated, stood at one side of the cabin, covered with a piece of green burlap, and used as a window seat. It was an ignominious end to a praiseworthy invention.

After luncheon Jane began at the wood pile. The way to do a thing, she always argued, was simply to do it. So now the way to develop muscle sufficient to cut down a tree was to begin on the wood pile.

The ax was sharp and of ordinary weight.

Any one could cut wood with that. Such work was mere play and muscle was to be developed by the pound.

After an hour's play with the ax, Jane decided it must be almost dinner time, even though the sun was so high in the heavens. But the wood pile! How strange! If there had been any one near her, Jane would have felt certain that they had played a joke on her by carrying off her wood as she cut it. To have worked the entire afternoon with only those few pieces of wood to show for it! Still, you never could tell. Wood was so deceptive because it always lay crosswise, piled up helter-skelter, piece tilted over piece like a pile of overturned jackstraws. Perhaps it would be better to pile the wood and then cut more. Change of work was recreation.

It took a surprisingly short time to pile that wood neatly in the corner at the side of the big fireplace. She had wanted to have the wood pile entirely out of doors but Burnham had warned her that sometimes the snows were deep. He had not the courage to tell her, so soon, how deep they sometimes were. So in the square set aside for the wood pile, she laid her newly cut wood. But there was so little of it!

She glanced at the clock. Just a little after three! And her hands! She had put on gloves for chopping but found it was a little dangerous because she could not control the ax. She had forgotten to put them on to carry in the wood and now her hands were full of splinters.

She would get accustomed to it, of course. These things all came by practice. She set aside the ax and picked up a small hatchet with which to cut some of the small dry branches which covered the ground. The new wood was too green to burn well. The rest of the afternoon she hacked at dry branches.

Next morning Jane slept late. Even when she did awaken, she felt a strange reluctance to getting up. She decided when dressing that it would be better to omit wood chopping that day. There was a slight attempt at trail clearing, but by noon she had given it up. That afternoon, warm in the sunlight, she sat by the side of the creek, reading a novel.

It was just before her evening dinner that she heard far down the trail, Burnham's yodel,

"He-e-e-e-igh ho-o-o-o!" With a quick jump, she revived the kitchen fire. An additional log went into the embers of the fireplace. Lack of hospitality in the woods was not easily forgiven. She felt sure he would get his supper at the Widdy's but she would give him a welcome.

Burnham sprang off his horse with a cordial greeting.

"How are things going? All right?"

"Yes, indeed. I did some clearing yesterday —see how much I did! And then I chopped some wood—all that in the corner. I had lots of fun!"

"But the fun was all *yesterday!*" His jolly laugh rang out cheerily.

"Ye-es. But I am learning how."

"I am going back to Illahee Monday. Shall I send out a man?"

"Perhaps—you might. It is so near winter— yes, I think it would be better. Of course, if I had come earlier or had begun earlier, I could do it all myself."

"Of course," he assented gravely.

"See what I 've brought you," he added, motioning toward a Boston terrier which had been sniffing around Jane. "Salt will be good company for you, I think." He avoided any further mention of danger.

"Salt!"

"His master called him that because he looked so much like pepper. Can you whistle?"

A whistle, clear but somewhat uncertain, was his answer.

"You can learn that, too; and it won't stiffen you up like chopping wood. I must go over to the Widdy's. I 'll leave Bob here if you will let me. He does n't like that stream any too well. I hope she 'll have some doughnuts," he added with a twinkle in his eye.

Jane turned her attention to the new dog.

An hour later Jack Burnham mounted Bob again, after a moment's chat in the dusk. "I think you can expect a man Tuesday," was his last word. "The Widdy wants some wood cut, too."

But there were days and days that glorious October when Jane with her hatchet hacked and chopped at the bushes and grubbed for the entangling vines which sprang from nowhere, and picked up chips for her fires, or stacked

together the dead branches of trees, and chopped
off the projecting ends of fallen trees until she
had cleared a patch, broad though bumpy, between the cabin and the creek. The man whom
Burnham sent out had made cord wood of the
old tree which had lain across that trail.

Then she turned her attention to a trail from
the cabin up the creek toward the pond, which
was really a momentary broadening out of the
mountain stream, and which lay just beyond the
boundaries of her claim. She was well over her
stiffness now, and the open-air exercise had not
only developed some of the longed-for "muscle"
but had brought a glow of color into her face
which had been unknown to Jane the school
teacher. The dead branches of the fallen trees,
brittle and dry, gave her a good fire, and would
serve well until the greener wood, recently cut,
could dry somewhat. But it could not all be
used and in a perfectly safe place, near the edge
of the creek, she used to burn her brush in the
most approved way. Goss had happened along
one day when she had started such a blaze and
in friendly fashion he had given her the necessary warning as well as instruction regard-

ing its management. He was friendly, in his quiet way, but he did not join her in the easy fashion which made Burnham such good company.

The presence of the dog, too, made a difference. He was always at her heels wherever she went, and grew to be an actual companion. And with the sense of responsibility for him— even to pulling out porcupine quills, as she had to one day,—the sense of blank loneliness had disappeared. A womanly woman has to have something for which she feels responsible else existence becomes gray. And Salt was a jolly companion. He chased the squirrels and when they barked at him, outraged and defiant, from the rough red bark of the firs, just above his wildest jump, he barked back until the forest echoed to the quarrel.

Hacking away one day at the brush on the trail to the lake, Salt, sitting on his haunches beside her gave a deep growl. Jane glanced up. There was nothing to be seen but Salt rose, growled more deeply, and showed his teeth. Man or animal, something was near. Jane slipped the leash around the dog's collar and rose to her full height. There was nothing to be seen in the silent morning,—only the sunshine playing on the red, seamy bark of the firs, and the ferns swaying slightly in the never-resting breeze. But the slight breeze, she realized with a start, did not account for the sudden swaying of bushes some fifty feet away. Tense, Jane watched them closely. Again a sudden swaying as though some heavy body had moved through them, or settled down among them. Salt growled again. Was it a bear? They were more likely to be in the huckleberry patches. A cougar? Or—or—a sudden picture came to her mind of the figure watching her from the spruce trees in the old burn. Could it be the squatter? Salt began to bark.

Jane felt for her revolver. "If it's that man, I am going to find out what he wants. I won't be watched in this way. Come, Salt."

They advanced slowly some twenty feet toward the clump of ferns and bushes. The agitated waving of the green brush was never occasioned by any breeze. Salt was barking loudly and Jane's finger was on the trigger. A still more violent shaking of the bushes and a tattered figure rose before her.

"Who are you and what do you want?" demanded Jane, feeling her knees shaking and conscious of a vague wonder in the back of her mind as to whether she would dare shoot a human being.

There was no answer.

"What are you doing here? Be quiet, Salt." Still no answer.

"Who are you? Do you live in that tree stump down there?" The revolver waved toward the south.

"Yes." The answer came slowly.

"What do you want here?" Jane looked as bravely as she could at the human scarecrow.

"I want you to understand," she went on as silence was her only response, "that this is my claim and that you have no business whatever on my homestead. You must keep off of it."

She was somewhat emboldened by his apparent fear.

"That's painters in thet thar ravine," he mumbled. "Yer better watch out."

[173]

"Painters—cougars? In what ravine?"

A dirty hand protruding from a tattered sleeve pointed toward the other corner of her claim.

"Are there cougars on my claim?" She was trying to see the squatter's face. Wild eyes, a dense bushy beard in a face browned by the sun, the whole appearance caricatured by the tattered clothing and crownless hat, she could make out nothing except that he was rather a fearsome-looking creature. He was evidently a fugitive. His furtive, watchful air, his neglected appearance, all gave evidence to that. But her common sense told her that any man as dirty and neglected and in similar clothes would look about as disreputable. She couldn't tell in the least whether he looked like a criminal or not.

"Have you seen the cougars?" But the squatter was moving off, with Salt straining at his leash to get at him. Jane watched him go with a sense of relief as he shambled through the underbrush and vanished amidst the trees. A big fir seemed to blot him out. She watched for his further movements, but there were none.

"Stopping behind that fir, I guess. He's

[174]

horrible looking but I am glad I had the courage to face him. I wish he would go on."

She turned back to her cabin and crossed the bridge to the Widdy's. Mrs. Patton was sewing on a patchwork quilt.

"Do you know anything about the man?" she asked as she finished telling of her encounter. "Has he ever come around here before?"

"Not sence I ben here. But he's no harm. He's too afeard," was the Widdy's answer.

CHAPTER XI

"BROOKSIDE"

Letter from Hope Denham to Jane Myers.

Dear Jane:

I am glad I 'm not up in those dense forests! Goodness! And with a forest fire possible eight months in the year! No, thank you. And it must be awfully lonely in there under all those great trees with the "dim forest gloom" that poets are so fond of talking about.

I have been having some experiences here, too. This is the last day of October and this past month has been ages long. There was a girl named Winters who came out here to visit Miss Woods—you remember I told you Miss Woods had the claim about a quarter of a mile from me. They used to teach in the same school. Miss Woods is awfully nice—about thirty, I guess. Well, this Miss Winters came out here because of nervous exhaustion, but, dear me, Jane, if she were to exhaust all her nerve, she would be so shrunk there would n't be anything left.

Jack Strong comes over to see me—you met him, did n't you?—and sometimes he goes to see Miss Woods. It's attentions without intentions, you know, because we neighbors have to be friendly out here on these great plains. Well, anyway, she found out he came here rather often because he's a special friend of Uncle Mart's,—oh, yes, I have named my claim "Brookside"; is n't that pretty?—and promptly this awful Miss Winters set her cap for him. I'm not jealous—you understand that! Because we 're just good friends, but he is good-looking you know, big and strong and broad-shouldered, and—and dependable, you* know. He makes me think of the *Virginian,* and I guess that's why I like him so much. So she began to come over here Sunday evenings when she knew he was here—*so busy* keeping house during the week. And then one night she announced she could sing. Of course we asked her to, because you have to be polite, even if you are homesteading. Then she wanted me to accompany her on my mandolin. She plays the guitar, and she really does have a good voice and a repertoire of clever pieces, and Jack—that is, Mr. Strong—Uncle Mart always says Jack —liked it very much. That was her cue. She just sang at all times and places. She came over twice a week to "practice" with me—in spite of that heavy housekeeping for two. And one day, when we were all out horseback riding—we four with Uncle Mart went on a picnic to a pretty spot twenty miles away just at the beginning of the foothills,—and, oh, Jane, it was the most glorious day! It had rained a little the night before and with the light breeze from the mountains, and the freshness of the air, the glorious October sunshine and magnificent blue sky above us, and, those boundless, endless, limitless plains behind us,—it was just beyond words. And we did have such a good time. But you know Miss Winters is *very* fond of music—*very*. Why, she got off her horse in front of a barbed-wire fence and sang all the dots on her veil! I did hear once of a girl who put a peek-a-boo waist in a piano player and the thing ground out a Beethoven sonata. I almost believe this Miss Winters could get Lohengrin out of a pair of

open-work stockings! Well, anyway, we had a
perfectly glorious day.

This Miss Winters told me once, apropos of
her housekeeping that she always kneaded
bread with her gloves on. I told her I needed
bread with my sweater on, but she did n't see the
joke at all—it was n't musical. Well, she 's
gone now. Her parting joke *was* musical.
Sampson was purring in front of the fire and she
said the cat had begun to boil!

I go over real often to see Miss Woods, and
so does Jack. He 's sorry for her because of
her health—but do you know, I believe it 's
rather a relief to him that Miss Winters 's gone.
It certainly is to me. But of course I was n't
jealous. She was just disagreeable. Miss
Woods is awfully lonely, and I guess Miss Winters's visit did mean a good deal to her. This is
her third year on her claim and her courage
seems to be going. They say that the last year
is sometimes the longest one, but I can't see how
that would be. Mine—I mean my first one—
was ages long. Uncle Mart had an Irishman
helping him a while this last summer, and the
Irishman was much interested in a woman's tak-

ing up a homestead. He said the whole thing was a bet: "Th' Guvermint is willin' to bet ye a hundred an' sixty acres uv land agin fourteen dollars thot ye can't live on it foive year widout starvin' to death."

There might be a little truth in that for some people, but not for me. I 'll stick to this place until my five years are up. Then, maybe, I will visit city sights again. I hope Miss Woods won't give up her claim. I 'm going to do everything I can for her—and Uncle Mart does, too. Oh, yes! That Miss Winters's first joke about the cat was that the way to make a Maltese cross was to step on the cat's tail—just because Sampson is part Maltese!

I have n't had a letter from you in ages. Do write, because you can't be so busy up there in those dense forests as I am cultivating my ground here, even if you do put on a flannel gym suit once in a while and pull up brush. Why don't you just wear overalls? I should think that would be all right up there,—there are so few men and those just forest rangers. Nobody you care anything about. I should think it would be all right to wear overalls. Of

course I would n't want to do that here. Mr.
Strong pops in too unexpectedly, but you
have n't any Mr. Strong there. Uncle Mart
goes over for the mail—five miles away in another direction,—so I don't have to worry about
that.

I love you, Jane. I wish we could homestead
together.

Your harum-scarum friend,
HOPE DENHAM.

P. S. I am going to get a cow. I never
milked one in my life, but I 've had *lots* of experience with fountain pens.

CHAPTER XII

HUNTING

NO sound had broken the stillness of the entire day. Under a dull sky, after a week of gloom, Jane was beginning to feel isolated. Some days she felt that the forest had withdrawn itself from her. It seemed wrapped in impenetrable mystery. Silence seemed to have settled over the mountain sides, even though there was always the crashing of Thunder Creek as it passed her cabin. She had thought that there was always a murmur in the forest. Sometimes when she dropped down quietly on the trail, or sat on the Douglas fir looking into the maze of green on the forest side, she had become conscious of an almost inaudible scurrying among the salal and fern brakes, a quivering of the crimson berries of the kinnikinnick, of the soft light patter of soft little feet, and sometimes, but especially at evening, she could hear the faint, lonely cry of the loon. But that was only when the stream had been lower. It was higher now, through recent rains. She imagined that in the very heart of the forest there might be absolute stillness, though at the edge of Thunder Creek and the tiny clearings around the cabins there had been a light flutter and ripple and rustling, evidence of life and action among the alder saplings and the spruces, for leaves and branches and treetops and torrent kept up incessant movement. But under the gray sky everything seemed quieter.

She sat mending a three-cornered tear this afternoon of early November, thinking of the old proverb: "Wherever a man dwells, he is sure to have a thorn bush near his door." The thorn bush this winter was going to be the isolation. That was clear. The Widdy might be some protection but she certainly was no company.

Jane stirred the fire for heat and opened the door for light. She looked up again at the gray, somber sky. Then her eye caught a movement far down the trail. She watched anxiously for a moment until she heard the yodel, already growing familiar. Burnham was the one man

[183]

who dropped in on his way up and down the trail, but this seemed to be some one else. As he came nearer he waved his hat. A moment later she recognized the ranger. He sprang off his horse and dropped the bridle to the ground.

"I know it's a little late," he said a little apologetically, after greetings had been exchanged, "but I wondered if you would care to go hunting. We are so busy now, cutting trails before the snow flies, that I cannot take a full day off."

"Are there calling hours in the forest? Come in."

He studied her face a moment as he entered the cabin and seated himself. He wondered if she were angry about the cutting of the Douglas fir. He himself never saw the splendid tree lying on the earth without a sense of regret, and yet a sense of relief. Jane studied him.

"Dear me! How shall I talk to him? What shall I say? If I am silent or quiet he will think me angry." Her thoughts flew from one subject to another, as a possible outlet for conversation. She never had any trouble in talking with Burnham. Yet her chief fear with this man was lest he should think her inhospitable. She suc-

ceeded in making a few aimless remarks, until
he spoke again of hunting.

"Yes, indeed. I should enjoy it. Is it far?
Is there hunting right around here?"

"There are pheasants and deer. I suppose
you have discovered there is fishing in the lake
above."

"The Wid—er—Mrs. Patton—said there was.
I went fishing there one day."

"Catch anything?"

"No-o."

"Perhaps you did n't have the right bait."

"I did n't stay very long. It was so quiet and
so lonely I could n't stand it."

"We 'll go fishing with you some day—Burnham or I." His fine, strong face had softened
at her confession. He picked up her gun and
examined it. He noted that it was in good condition.

"This is all right for large game."

"You mean for deer. I never could shoot a
deer,—never. I saw a deer's eyes once after it
was shot. I 'd rather starve than kill one myself."

"It is almost murderous to kill them merely

[185]

for sport, or merely for the head and horns. But where one shoots them for food—the only fresh meat we have out here—is it any worse than fishing? Or shooting pheasants?"

"But fish never look at you in that human way, or pheasants, either."

"Do you want to take my fowling piece and let me take your gun? I started out with the idea of shooting pheasants."

The gun question settled, with another log on the fire to keep it until their return, they started off. Goss led the way, stepping surely as though following a trail, though to Jane the forest looked, as it always did, like an impenetrable tangle. There could be but little talk except a few words now and then, as he held back a branch which might strike her in the face, pointed out an unusual clump of sword ferns waving high over some old decayed log, its former trunk a mere shell of rotten wood ready to sink under the lightest step. Jane was a fairly good mountaineer. With flannel waist of gray-blue, high boots which met at the knee her short dark-blue skirt (Bert Fairfax had warned her against ever wearing brown during the hunting season), and a soft felt hat, she moved lightly over log bridges, or sprang from rock to rock over some small brook with a steady footing which made the walk a pleasure to her companion. The ranger, less artistic but none the less practical in his dress, looked like many another hunter until he turned and she caught the pleasant lines in his face and the pleasant light in the steady gray eyes.

"We might have brought the dog," said Goss suddenly as they paused near the edge of the creek.

"He 's lost—I don't know where. I can't find him." Her voice was distressed.

"Lost! How?"

"I don't know. One day I was digging around a little, cutting at salal bushes, when he began to chase a squirrel. The squirrel ran from one tree to another in the most provoking way, and then I heard Salt far off, barking in the strangest way. I had never heard him bark like that before. And then there was some other sound—I can't tell what it was. It sounded almost as if—as if—I can't express it. But it frightened me so that I jumped up and ran into

[187]

the house, though I left the door open after a minute for Salt. But he did n't come. Then I took my gun and went out to the corner of the house and whistled for him the longest while. There was n't a sound and I have n't seen him since."

Goss stood looking down upon her gravely.

"I am sorry," he said very gently. "It was a real loss for you."

"I felt like such a coward. I do yet. If poor Salt was attacked by some wild animal I ought to have gone to his rescue. Don't you think so?"

"No, indeed," he answered emphatically. "Indeed I do not. You did the very thing you should have done."

"Run into the cabin and shut the door and shake like a leaf? It was cowardly. And I 'm lonely without the dog."

The ranger's sympathetic manner had made the girl forget her awe of him.

"It is possible," he explained, "that some wild animal attacked Salt; more possible, I think, that Salt attacked the wild animal first and brought about his own destruction. I'm sorry he's gone. A dog is jolly good company. But you did right not to follow him."

He had almost forgotten pheasants until his eye caught sight of one, a mass of gray feathers, close up against the trunk of a small spruce tree whose low branches brought the bird well within range. He pointed it out to Jane. She raised her gun and aimed it, but her hands were trembling. Goss stepped backward in order not to distract her. *Bang!* went the gun. The pheasant flapped its wings and flew into the forest.

"Oh," exclaimed Jane, crimson with mortification. She realized that she had shut her eyes when she fired.

The ranger's face was perfectly grave.

"Any one might have missed it," he said quietly. "It was very close to the trunk."

"You wouldn't have missed it." She had no wish to defend herself.

"I had a funny experience in the Maine woods one autumn," he laughed. "A party of us were out, including one young woman who couldn't shoot as well as you can. She was with me and we both aimed for a pheasant at the same moment. When we picked up the bird, we could see at a glance that both our shots had not taken effect. She fairly shouted with exultation: 'I shot it! I shot it! You missed!' It never entered her mind for two years after, as she herself told me, that she might have missed it and I shot it."

The deep pleasant voice as they walked on was pitched low for fear of disturbing possible game, but some sound caused a stir in a clump of young Christmas trees. Goss fired as a startled brown head was lifted above the bushes. Something fell. Both ran forward but Goss reached the spot first and called back:

"Don't come, Miss Myers. It's—er—venison."

They reached the cabin in high spirits, for a venison dinner and good company would take off the edge of isolation for days to come.

Goss carved out a generous share for the Widdy. "I don't know where she will keep it, though," he added as he started for the door.

"I know where I am going to keep mine,"

said Jane triumphantly. "I shall hang it up in my screen pen."

"And bring all the cougars in the forest down around your cabin?" He started out of the door.

When he returned, Jane felt again her sense of awe of him. He, in turn, was silent also.

The venison dinner was not a very gay one.

"Do you think you're going to like it here?" he asked at last, glancing around the cozy little room.

"Yes, indeed."

"The snows are deep in winter, you know. You will be shut in."

"I shall be happy here. I am positive of that."

"Do you know the definition of 'positive'?" He was smiling now.

"Absolutely certain, is n't it?"

"Some one defined it as 'being mistaken at the top of your voice.'"

"Perhaps I shall be bored. But I was so tired of teaching. Do you ever get tired of your work?"

"I love it. It means so much to me."

"I should think you would get tired of the rough life—or is n't it rough?" she added, half timidly, hoping that she was not offending him.

"You love the beauty of the forests. I have heard you say so. Do you remember the view of the snow-capped peak towering high over the valley and the rounded lower mountains, on the road as you came out?"

"Yes, indeed."

"Can you imagine what that scene would be if instead of these magnificent forests, green and fresh, bending and swaying and murmuring in the breeze, far below you, and above you as well—what that scene would be if instead it were merely thousands of acres of mountain side covered with charred and hideous stumps?"

Jane began to gather up the dishes. Goss rose and stood by the hearth, leaning against the primitive mantle.

"Our work," he went on, "is to care for the forests. Theoretically it is not simply fire fighting, but practically, under the present conditions, it is. But it 's the old story of an ounce of prevention. The way to fight fires is to prevent them from starting. We try to protect exposed borders from fires among rubbish left in logged-off lands—"

"Those logged-off lands are fearful. They are blots and scars on the face of nature."

"Some lands, useful for agriculture, ought to be logged off, you know. Then when the stumps are disposed of by burning or pulling out, you have land of high value. But I mean where the land is simply stripped of its timber and left to go to ruin, with piles of débris which ought to be burned and are not. Usually such lands are near a railroad or on a logging road, and sparks catch in the dry tinder. They begin to smolder, a light blaze comes and the flames sweep up into the standing timber on a near-by hillside—perhaps into a reserve or a national park. If we can protect the borders of the forest from fires among débris, and from fires in slashings, we can keep the mountain sides forested. Otherwise,—perhaps not."

"I noticed in coming into the mountains in August," Jane answered, "that along the tracks piles of old ties were burning. The valleys were full of thick blue smoke, cutting off all view, and in some places the fire from the ties had run through the dry bushes and set fire to trees. Section hands were around, watching the fires I suppose, but they did not seem to be doing anything to put them out."

"They take it for granted they will burn out before a breeze springs up. The railroads are one of our worst enemies on fires. Besides burning their ties at the driest time of the year, the engines on the upgrade emit volcanoes of sparks. That starts a good many fires. Spark arresters partially prevent that, but they cut off power from the engine, too. They ought to burn oil. Lightning starts some fires, and the sheep men start them—"

"Why?"

"They want more pasturage. Campers start a lot of fires by pure carelessness—start fires against dead logs and leave them smoldering. Throw cigars and cigarette ends in dry brush and leave them there to go out or to start a little piece of dry humus to smoldering. Then a breeze springs up—and away goes a smart blaze up into the timber. Miners and prospectors are sinners, as well. Loggers burn their slashings in dry summer weather—same story."

"Is n't there some law about slashings?"

"That they be burned,—yes. But they should be burned only in late fall or in the early spring. Some day the loggers and railroads will have to come to time—but we can't control the lightning yet."

Jane had piled the dishes up on the broad board which she, like many others, used as a kitchen table. Goss paced up and down the small room, while she dropped into the smaller rocker.

"You were trained in the forestry school, were n't you?" she asked at length.

"Yes. That's where Burnham and I learned to know each other. Burnham is a fine fellow. My family do not like my profession, though. Mother wanted me to be a lawyer, and my sister cannot understand why I enjoy looking and living like a tramp, as she expresses it. She's rather fond of social life. But I don't expect to be a ranger always," he added. "I was a little slow in getting started, thanks to an A. B.,

[195]

and then a try at law, and then the forestry school. Then Mother and Madge wanted to go abroad and could n't go without a man. Finally, we arranged it so that Madge did the cathedrals, and I studied European forestry methods. Mother vibrated between us until she is reasonably certain, I think, that Westminster cathedral is in the middle of the Black Forest. So I was twenty-seven before I came out here."

Jane did some rapid figuring. This was his second year as ranger, she knew. So he was twenty-nine. He looked a little older. She had put him down for thirty or thirty-one.

"And your promotion?"

"I understand that I am slated for deputy supervisor of this reserve within a few months— oh, possibly it may be delayed until next summer. But I need this experience if I am to manage other rangers. I can gauge their work better."

"What does a forestry school teach?"

Goss had become unusually talkative. Jane decided that the best way to interest him was to keep him talking about his work. He did not answer directly as he paced up and down the

[196]

room, stopping now and then to lean against the mantle and look down at her. Outside the gray afternoon was dimming into twilight.

"The examination for ranger is the funniest thing you ever saw. Part of it is practical, you know. A man is given a mixed-up assortment of frying pans, blankets, tin plates and cups, axes, coffeepots, shovels, provisions, clothing, ropes, and anything that is necessary, and told to fasten them on a horse's back for a trip into the mountains. You can imagine such an array on a tricksy little cayuse that will have to climb, swing, slide, jump,—yes, and wade,—through streams and over steep roads barred by logs and sometimes almost impassable. You see such a test shows his ability to make a hitch that will hold—and when a man loses his coffeepot ten miles from another one, it's food for reflection even if no hot drink for his other self."

He paced the floor a few minutes and suddenly stopped by her chair.

"What do you do here all by yourself?"

"Mend and sew, cook and keep house, and read—and write letters. Sometimes I grub around the bushes and cut out vines that may

trip me up on the trail to the creek—and sometimes I dream dreams and see visions."

"Do you?"   His whole face lighted up, as he
added mentally: "You're all right then.   I
thought you might be a man hater."   His keen
glance studied her face.   Why should a woman
like this take up a homestead in the forest?   He
was certain that there was a love affair back of
it somewhere,—"even if her name is Jane," he
added to himself, smiling at a certain recollection.

"I don't mean to be curious," he said aloud,
"but I cannot understand why a woman should
take up a claim in such an isolated place.   It's
natural to think of her in a home."

Jane flushed.   He was on that tack, was he!!

"I was thoroughly tired of teaching," she said
with a certain indifference in her tone,—"thoroughly tired of it—and—and I think every
woman has a right to live her own life.   That
is, make the most of herself."

"And you think you are making the most of
yourself out here—with the Widdy and the
bears?"

She started to say "And you and Mr. Burnham," but caught herself as she remembered she was indebted to Bert Fairfax for their attentions.

"Why not?" she answered. "I have more time for reading than I ever had before—more time for thinking—more exercise."

"How about other people? And it's for five years, you know."

He was beating around that same old circle again. She could almost hear Bert Fairfax say, in his frank, honest way, "Jane, why don't you marry?"

"Tell me something more about your work." She was anxious to change the subject. "What are the plans for this reserve?"

"We are only one reserve in many." The smile left his face. He felt a little disappointed in the girl. "Take all the reserves together and the government is planning something like thirty thousand miles of trail—that includes pack trails and blazed trails, both,—some sixteen thousand miles of telephone wire, and about seven thousand miles of good, passable roads. But Congress cuts down the appropriations to such an extent that heaven only knows when we will get all this. And we need it—need it des-

perately—if we are to save the forests. Tell me
what you dream about."

He was standing in the chimney corner now,
looking down at her. The tall, finely built
figure leaned forward a little with a certain
earnestness. Then suddenly realizing how he
towered above her, he sat down in the other
rocker and turned the chair so he could face her.

Jane answered a little guardedly.

"I have learned an immense amount of salt
folklore since I came out here," she laughed.
"I have found out that salt is the remedy for
everything evil—why did n't I think of that before?"

"Of what?"

"Putting salt on that pheasant's tail. It
would have saved me the mortification of seeing
the bird flap its wings and fly off. I know that
joke is a trite one—or used to be. But with the
Widdy's ideas, I see it in a new light. And I
have learned, from a friend of mine who has
access to a library, that witches are fond of lurking under alder trees—and just think of all the
alder trees which border Thunder Creek. But
the bracken will break the spell if you cut the

root the right way, because at the joints you will find the letter C. Also holly is fatal to witches, and I think the Oregon grape ought to be. It is the holly-leaved barberry. Sue Fairfax is getting to be an expert in witchcraft lore, and I have lots of fun about the Widdy with her. Of course, I don't think the Widdy really believes in witches, but she is always guarding against invisible evils; therefore her quantities of salt. But then, I 've had experiences, too."

"What kind?"

"I 've seen nixies when I went to get water. And once when I was sitting perfectly still on a trunk, I saw some of the moss people. They are the same size as little children but very gray and old-looking, hairy and dressed in moss. Once, in the moonlight, I caught a glimpse of Queen Mab."

"Did you go out in the moonlight alone?"

"Yes. I had forgotten to bring in fresh water."

"Don't do it, please. It is n't safe."

There were two very striking things about Leonard Goss, and his request brought out both of them. Jane took her turn in looking at him

as she studied over the matter a moment. He
was a man who commanded as a matter of
course. And he expected to be obeyed. Yet
there was nothing dictatorial in his voice, and
he possessed a wonderful gentleness of manner.
Jane remembered a remark her mother often
made:—that a man who is truly strong is always
the gentlest of men. Especially with women,
easily crushed by such strength, are they defer-
ential. His request had been made in the pleas-
antest way, in the kindest manner; yet it was a
command and she recognized it as such without
resentment.

"Do you never dream of people when you
dream dreams?" he asked. He was wondering
whether there were any man-hating propensities
in this capable, energetic girl. She answered
guardedly again:

"I see visions for all my friends. I feel sure
Mrs. Fairfax's Teddy will be a philosopher.
Sue has two beautiful children. You know
Mr. Fairfax, don't you?"

"I have just met him—through Mr. Burnham. That is all."

"Then I have another friend who is a home-

steader, near the foothills in Colorado. She is
the one who inspired me. I dream about Hope
—and her friend."

"She is engaged?"

"She was—yes, she is."

"She has n't broken it?"

Little enough Goss cared about the friend's
friend. He was trying to study out the woman
before him.

"I don't know. She's very impetuous—and
her letter is not very clear. But I have dreamed
about both of them and how happy they are
going to be."

The strong face relaxed. She was n't a man
hater, then,—even if some love affair had driven
her into the wilderness. She was independent
enough, but there were no apparent distortions
of view. The ranger was hardly conscious of
his own thoughts, or where they were leading
him.

"You must remember one thing,"—and he
rose to go. "The snows here are deep sometimes, although the winters are never severely
cold. Many a winter it does not reach anywhere near zero. But you must fill your house

[203]

here with plenty of wood. That is absolutely necessary."

"It will clutter up my cabin."

"Never mind that. The crowding will steadily diminish after the cold and snow come. Fill up your extension also, and use that first."

"I 'd rather use that last."

"Impossible. Use the wood from out-of-doors first; save this inside for emergencies."

Jane looked up at him. He almost dictated to her. Why could he never remember it was her cabin and not his?

Perhaps he caught her thought, or perhaps he was recalling winter experiences, for he looked down upon her very thoughtfully. He knew something of what was before her. Jane suddenly realized again that the gray eyes could be exceedingly kind.

It was only late afternoon, yet dark, when Dick trotted down the trail. Goss looked back as he began to wind among the trees and his face lighted up again as he saw the girlish figure silhouetted in black against the bright light of the cabin. Then the door closed and all was dark.

"She's plucky, all right, Dick. If she can pull through this first winter, she'll win."

He fell into a brown study, letting the canny horse pick his own way, but just before he reached the main trail his trained ear caught from somewhere the far-off cry of a cougar.

"I was afraid of it, Dick," he said aloud.

He was perfectly certain then as to what had become of poor Salt.

As Jane turned back to the fire, she took again a much-read letter from her workbasket. It was in a different tone from Hope's buoyant one.

Dear Jane:

I have had the most *harrowing* experience this last week. I am so upset. I have suddenly discovered that Jack Strong is the *brother* of Mac, my old principal. Can you imagine anything more unexpected? It seems that they were both very small children when their mother married again and Mac took his stepfather's name. Jack was the elder and he liked the ring of his own name so well that he wouldn't give it up.

Really, it has upset me. I don't hate Mac, even though I did have such a time with him, for you know I have always felt Mrs. Mac was much to blame for his distorted views of things. When a man *is* prejudiced, you know, he is a good deal worse than a woman. She talked so much that it was from her half-statements, I have been told, there grew up all those exaggerated stories about my defying him and telling him I would wear crape to school if I wanted to. I have Mrs. Mac to thank for some very unpleasant gossip. And if Jack insists that I shall go right into his family and subject myself to his sister-in-law's ungenerous tongue, we shall have to call it off. She does n't spare her dearest friends. Oh, dear! Why did they have to be brothers? Do write and give me some good advice, that 's a dear. I love Jack so dearly. And to have the shadow of this old annoyance come in, makes me sick.

Just now I 'm nothing but A forlorn
HOPE.

Jane studied the letter a long while. She had known of the difficulty at the time, had known of Mrs. Mac's share in it because she had called there one day when Mrs. Mac, not knowing of their intimacy, started to gossip with her about Hope. Mac was not an easy man to get along with. After one year of it, Jane had asked for a transfer.

Her mind drifted from Jack Strong to Jack Burnham and his cordial friendliness. She was beginning to feel that it was not all due to his friendship for Bert Fairfax. And this Mr. Goss—she studied over him for a long while. It was only when the fire log broke apart with a sputter and a shower of sparks that she aroused. "After all, Jane," she said as she wound the clock, "there are some pretty nice men in this world."

CHAPTER XIII

MY CABIN

FRESH snow had fallen during the night. Softly the flakes sifted down from the low-hanging clouds, covering everything with a clinging mantle of white. The green tops of the tall cedars were crowned with fleecy softness, and soft bits of the same white fleece transformed the wide-spreading branches of the spruces. The seamy ridges of the firs were softened and rounded into full curves by the white down which clung to them. In the clearings around the cabins snow lay a foot deep, though under the protecting trees the sword ferns pierced with their long green points their white covering. Nor had the weight of snow concealed altogether the glossy leaves of the salal bushes.

Jane opened the door to look out upon the first beauty of the day. The fresh color in her face and the clearness of the violet eyes told of the vigor which had come with days spent working in the open air. Behind her, the fire glimmered and crackled on the open hearth.

"Is n't it wonderful!" She had used that phrase so often this last autumn. Every month brought some new beauty. She looked at the tall firs and then at the spruces with their burdens of white. Toward the forest she could see the dark trunks black against the snow.

"This certainly is better than teaching school. And I can't see that it is going to be as uncomfortable as last winter in La Casa. Those sharp, icy blasts across the prairies—straight from the north pole. And the storms and drifts and half-frozen children and blown-in windows! Besides an uncomfortable boarding house! Oh, it's the woods for me. And it's my cabin and my land. Those glorious trees all belong to me—and just now they're getting ready for Christmas."

She looked at the stump of the Douglas fir. She would beautify that stump next spring. She would nail pieces of bark to it, fill in the hollow with rich earth from the woods and plant in it great sword ferns, filling in the bare spots with the dainty leaves of the red-berried kinnikinnick. She would redeem the loss of that fir so far as she could.

She looked again to where the mighty Douglas fir lay, its entire length covered with the soft white snow. Her eye followed the trunk to its upper end, free now from the green top which had withered and faded and dropped away in the fall. The branches of other trees and its own shattered branches, as well, lay piled in an unsightly heap near the trail.

"I 'll have that cleared away next summer. It is unsightly and it might be dangerous in case of fire. It 's so near the trail."

The practical side of things recalled her to herself. She put on the snowshoes which Burnham had sent out to her, and threw her shawl around her. She needed fresh water for coffee. Thunder Creek had risen, she knew, during the past few days. The water was swirling almost level with the bank in the deep pool from which she usually dipped it. She stood there a few moments watching the flecks of foam which swept by her, listening to its steady roar. On the other side of the creek she could see the footprints of some wild animal which had come down to drink during the night. She began to hum a little song.

The Widdy's door opened as she stood there and she waved her hand. The old woman acknowledged it with a half wave of hers and the door closed again.

"It's the forest for me," she exclaimed as she looked around her. "I love it. I love it."

Suppose the snow did get deeper. She had been told that it was very deep in midwinter in the higher mountains. But what did it matter! There was plenty of food, of firewood, of books and leisure to read them, sewing enough to vary the monotony, beautiful surroundings and scenery, good health, a chance for exercise on the snowshoes, nothing to worry about, and the companionship, such as it was, of a woman old enough and experienced enough to be a source of safety to her. Moreover, there were the two friends of Bert Fairfax's who had been so kind to her. What more could any one want?

Jane recalled the arguments which had been made against her taking up a homestead and the predictions of loneliness and unrest.

"It's the modern craving for something new," she explained to herself. "It's a sort of universal restlessness. And I love this beauty and quiet. I certainly can get along without people for one winter, anyway."

She almost tripped herself on her snow-shoes. She was not at all expert in managing them.

"There was Mrs. Winthrop. She went up into the mountains one winter with her husband and everybody told her she would go crazy with the loneliness and monotony after they were snowed in. They were shut in for five months and she said she never had a better time. She had leisure to read books she had waited half her life to read. Even *'Les Miserables!'* I asked for that once at the public library and they offered me three fat volumes—an armload. So I decided to wait to read it until I stopped teaching and could devote myself to it. Oh, I'm glad I came. Now I have my very own cabin. And I can plow through the snow far enough to get water."

She leaned over the creek to dip up a pail of water, but the toe of one clumsy snowshoe caught on a rock. Catching her balance, she dropped the bucket. "Gracious! I'll need to be more careful." She picked up the pail and bracing herself carefully, dipped up the water from the racing stream.

As she stood there, the sun came out. The air was soft—not at all cold. She knew that the cold was never intense in the Northwest. Bert had tried to explain the influence of the Japan current—or Japanese current, which was it? All she got out of it was the fact that the Northwest had an unusually temperate climate, summer and winter. So now as the gray clouds broke away and she could see the clear blue sky above, and the sunlight gleaming on the fresh whiteness of the snow, she hummed her little song again. What more could any one want?

"It's a good sign. A happy winter—snow outside, perhaps, but plenty of sunshine within. *Why* does the Widdy think the winters are so hard? She won't give me anything like a reason. And *why* did those two men urge me to go into town until spring? It's because they think I'm a tenderfoot! They don't realize what storms I faced last winter."

Still she stood there, looking up the creek and down, humming her little song and planning for the spring. She glanced at the Thunder Creek trail—so-called. It made her think of a fragment from some poem:

> "The path that seemed a twisted dream
> Where everything came true."

"Now *what* does that mean?" Jane gazed at the trail and meditated over the lines. The trail and the fragment seemed to fit, but just what did it mean?

"I 'm going to clear that trail next spring, also the one to the fishing pond above. I 'll need both, especially the fishing trail." The girl never dreamed how badly she would some day need that trail.

"I did n't suppose, Jane, that there would be work enough in one small cabin to keep a person busy all the time, but truly with your improvements you have n't wasted much time. I wish Sam was here. I 'd have a snowballing match with him."

Sam's company had been a real pleasure to the homesteader. With him she felt like going

further into the forest on short exploring ex-
peditions. Otherwise she liked to sit on a log
and look around her quarter section and remember it was all hers. All she had to do was to
"sit down on it," as that woman had said, for
five years, and improve it, according to law, of
course. She had been there nearly four months.
That was almost half a year. And it only took
the two halves to make a whole year.

The Widdy was an element of safety. She
considered it all, as she stood there. Monosyllabic Sam afforded a certain amount of companionship, and the two men who occasionally
came up the trail supplied the sense both of
protection and companionship. She did not
realize how much it meant to both of them to
step inside that cozy room with its feminine belongings, the sewing basket on the table, a book
with a handkerchief in it to mark the place,
pictures hung on the rough log walls against a
background of dull brown burlap. She did not
know that she was something of a study to them.
She thought she was doing all the studying of
character. And they were a study, those two.
Burnham, with his jolly laugh, his bright talk

and humorous turns of expression, and Goss
with his air of command and of protection, the
pleasant gray eyes that said so much even
though the lips were rather silent,—a man who
gave always the impression of strength. And
it was so especially nice that they were intimate
friends.

Jane wondered as she picked up her water
bucket and turned toward the cabin where they
were now. Burnham was probably in Illahee,
figuring on lumber, but Goss, she felt sure, was
up in the forest somewhere, loving the beauty
of it as she did. She recalled what he had said
once about protecting the deer from hunters
who shot out of season, and his half-vexed remark, "I wish hunters were half as fond of
shooting cougars and timber wolves as they are
deer."

Fifty feet from her cabin door, glancing up,
she was startled to see some wild animal sitting
on the upper half of the Douglas fir, watching
her. The animal was perhaps a hundred feet
from the cabin door. The door was open, too,
she remembered, as she stopped abruptly and
stared at the terrifying vision. It was a cougar,

—she was sure of that. The tawny back, the catlike face! She dropped the bucket of water and started on the run for the door. But she had forgotten the snowshoes and, quick as a flash, she tripped herself up and went down into the snow. The shawl tangled itself about her head. A wave of sickening fear took possession of her. Even without that wretched shawl, she might scream all day and not make the Widdy hear. She was done for! Perhaps she might get herself free from those clumsy snowshoes. She tried to free her arms and head from the entangling shawl, but it only made matters worse. As she struggled to get on her feet, something sharp caught her ankle. Was it the cougar? The shriek she gave was muffled in shawl and snow. But Jane determined to die hard and struck at the animal with the other shoe. She could feel long claws scratching her skin, cutting in deeper and deeper. Why did n't he kill her at once and be done with it! If only somebody would come! She struggled and floundered until finally with a desperate effort, in striking at the cougar, she freed herself from one snowshoe. Another effort and she got upon her feet, her hair all down and full of snow, the shawl wound around her neck, her eyes full of snow. But the cougar seemed to have retreated for a moment. Perhaps she might gain the cabin. She glanced cautiously about her. Perhaps it had gone into the open cabin door! Again that sickening sense of fear. Jane started again on a run, as well as she could, the free foot sinking deep into the soft snow, the other one striking her at every moment. The snow behind her was dripping with blood, she was certain, but she was so entangled in that confounded shawl she could not see anything. As she neared the cabin door, in this unequal struggle between the two feet, the snow partly brushed from her eyes, she looked again to the log where the animal had been.

The cougar was still there! But as she looked it rose, moving slightly its long, lithe body. It lifted one foot—and Jane burst in at her cabin door, sprawling full length on the floor as that wretched snowshoe again tripped her up. It was but a moment before she sprang up, expecting every second to see that tawny body springing in the door. She dropped the long wooden bar into its place with trembling hands, and herself into the nearest chair. When she had pulled herself together again, she stepped carefully to the nearest knife, and deliberately and viciously cut the lacings of the snowshoe. She had tied them on, around her ankles! It was such a relief to kick it into the corner. A glance at the broken frame explained the "clawing" she had received. She laughed, though half hysterically.

In her long stay at the creek, she had completely forgotten her breakfast. She forgot it still longer as she sat down, with two ordinary shoes clothing her feet and studied over the situation. No more snowshoes for her! Not if the snow was ten feet deep! She looked at her ordinary shoes with gratitude. She would trust to them, snow or rain. But the bacon, having fried to a beautiful brown, shrunk into black, burned bits. The graham gems were hard as rocks and black as cinders. Jane did not heed. The water for her coffee was somewhere on the trail between the cabin and the creek. She sat in the chair, looking at her feet, and considered. The bottom suddenly seemed

[219]

to have dropped out of everything. And all because a tawny cougar had sat on the end of a fir log that morning and watched her get a bucket of water.

CHAPTER XIV

CHRISTMAS

Letter from Jane Myers to Hope Denham.

Dear Hope:

I suppose you and Uncle Mart and Jack Strong and Miss Woods are planning all sorts of jolly good times for to-morrow. I don't believe it's half as lonesome homesteading on the plains as in the forest. At least you can see far, far away. But here everything is solemn and mysterious, and on a gray day the somberness fairly gets on my nerves. I sometimes wonder if I were perfectly wise in taking up this homestead—and then when the sun comes out, and the forest rangers—I mean Mr. Goss and Mr. Burnham—his name's Jack, too, I think I told you—come, why, then I know it is wise. Because I was so tired of teaching, and you know when you get a square peg in a round hole, it's hard on the hole as well as on the peg, and I do feel myself at home here—especially when the sun shines. Of course, I can't look four years and a half ahead and see what results are going to be, because you know results are what you expect but consequences are what you get. And there *are* times when I feel that the mountain range I should most enjoy would be a good-sized cook stove—withi reach of civilization.

You 'll think I am blue, but really I am not. I am very cheerful, indeed—smiling like Fortune, but Mr. Burnham said once that Fortune sometimes smiled because she had to, the circumstances were so ludicrous.

But will you believe it? I am here in my cabin, the day before Christmas absolutely and entirely alone—unless that squatter's around the woods somewhere.

Yesterday when I went to the creek to get some water, the Widdy opened her door and flagged me. We make signals, you know, because we could n't possibly hear over the rush of the water. But in spite of the crash of the creek, I could hear the wind muttering something to itself up in the treetops, and everything was a little gloomy. So I went over the bridge and she told me she was going into Illahee for Christmas. Her son-in-law was there, too,—though I had n't seen him come—he had come out for her and she is n't coming back for ten days. And I know Jack Burnham—Mr. Goss always calls him Jack and it seems more natural to speak of him that way, but I could n't *imagine* myself speaking of Mr. Goss as Leonard—is in the city, and heaven only knows where Mr. Goss is. Anyway, I don't, and I don't much care. He 's not the most sociable man on earth, though he does have a pleasant face, I 'll have to admit, and pleasant eyes. But anyway, he 'd never put himself out for me. So I 'm alone in the world, with just those horrible wood rats thumping over my cabin roof every night in their wild efforts to get in. Did you ever hear anything equal to the *thump! thump! thump!* of their feet!

So here I am, nine o'clock in the morning, with my housework all done and a perfect gale blowing outside. Mr. Burnham says that wind is air when it gets in a hurry. I can't go out if I want to, and it seems so awfully dreary I

don't want to. There's about a foot of snow
on the ground, but it is rather wet—we've had
no real cold weather yet. It has snowed off
and on, but I think it's going to be a very pleasant open winter. Only this wind! It's one of
those soft, warm, wet winds from the ocean—I
think they call it a Chinook—and it started to
blow last night—perhaps that's what the treetops were muttering about in the morning.
But all night it blew and blew and *blew!* And
this morning the snow was all slushy with little
rivulets everywhere, and the creek was a raging,
untamed, irresponsible rive—

Two o'clock.

Well, I got just that far, because I haven't
an earthly thing to do except to write you this
long spiel, when over the rush of the wind and
the roar in the trees and the thunder of the water, I heard a fearful crash. Everything in the
cabin shuddered and shook. You can see the
blot of ink. I thought of an earthquake, but
there wasn't any more shaking, so then I looked
out. What do you think? The fir nearest my
cabin, but almost on the creek edge, had fallen

down—blown down by the wind, I guess, the things are so shallow rooted—and the branches clear at the tip edge landed across our tree bridge! Maybe it did n't jar that bridge! I would n't dare cross it now even if the Widdy were here. And the water is rising in the creek bed and just whirling down.

I wonder if there 's any danger of a flood! I wish I had thought to ask whether it ever does overflow. But yet, I believe Mr. Goss would have warned me if there was. Jack Burnham might have forgotten it, or not wanted to frighten me, but I believe Mr. Goss would have told me straight out. He 's not so sensitive about hurting people's feelings—only I would n't care much about the feelings, if I just knew I was safe. I don't believe the water can touch me, because I am on higher land, yet I do feel worried. It 's dark and gray outside and the snow is still melting, and what will happen before to-morrow morning, *I* don't know.

Just the same, Jane will hang up her stocking at the chimney place and set out the presents she has made for herself and have a sure-enough Christmas, even alone. I have baked a plum pudding this week, and I shall have hot rolls, and salt mackerel for breakfast, and some smoked venison for dinner, and maybe a chafing dish omelet for supper. I saw such a good definition of a chafing dish the other day—a frying pan that's got into society. You see, all my Christmas presents,—and I suppose I have *some*—are at Illahee. The Widdy's son-in-law brought out no mail when he came because she was going back and he forgot me! I am going to spend the day making a taboret. Thank goodness I like to hammer and nail and pound! I inherited that taste from my father. And I have his liking for whittling, too. Mother used to tell me about him.

Do you know, I can't make up my mind whether this sort of a life makes a woman strong-minded or weak-minded—one never hears of anything in between. We learn to be so mighty independent, and yet when you run up against the elemental forces of primitive nature, as one does in the forest here,—men are, well,—conveniences, anyway. And I am beginning to understand why past generations were perfectly willing to accept merely a woman's privileges and let the men have all the rights. I don't believe I ever was very strong on woman's rights, anyway, but I'm beginning to get another view of things from that seen by city women.

There is n't one bit of fun in this letter, Hope, but I can't seem to be jolly to-day. The Widdy told me once that the way to cure a boy of homesickness was to put salt in the hem of his trousers and make him look up the chimney. If I only had those overalls you preach about! But I should scandalize all right thinking people, I am sure, if I were to regard my gym suit as trousers and they're the nearest thing I have. So that remedy won't work with me—and I forgot for the moment I was n't a boy.

I read an odd quotation yesterday, from some old Anglo-Saxon source, I think. "The flood wave and the swift ebb tide; what the flood wave brings you in, the ebb sweeps out of your hand." What *does* it mean? Do you think it means that as soon as I prove up on this claim— after five years of life in the forest—that something, perhaps a forest fire, will sweep it all away? I wish I had n't read the old thing.

Do write to me when you can. I *need* letters.

Affectionately,

JANE.

P. S. Don't be anxious about the wrinkles on your cow's horns. They are not caused by worry.

P. S. 2. I had n't sealed the envelope, so I 'll add this note. It 's about ten o'clock, and it 's a fearful night outside. The rumble and roar and crash and thunder of the wind and water,—did I ever tell you there was a fifty-foot fall about six hundred feet down the trail—and the way in which the water dashes over that, why, I can't hear myself think, even on bright days. But now! The tumult outside is *fearful,* and every once in a while there is a sort of crackling sound, and the cabin shakes—trees going down in the wind, I suppose. I barred my doors and windows hours ago, but I can hear the rush and swish of the rain on the glass —my shutters are inside the cabin, are yours? —and the wet splashes down my chimney and hisses in the fire. It 's a wild night! And tomorrow 's Christmas. Goodness. How I wish

you were here—you, or the Widdy, or Jack
Burnham, or even Mr. Goss. Just anybody for
company!

Letter from Jane Myers to Hope Denham.

Dear Hope:

I wrote you a letter the day before Christmas and sealed it, but it's still on the shelf over
the fireplace. Mr. Goss is asleep over in the
Widdy's cabin and so I'll write you the rest
of the story of the flood. The excitement's all
over now.

Christmas morning,—I didn't get much
sleep that night, I can promise you,—I got up
early. And why in the world I did it, I don't
know, but I put on my gym suit. Even now
I couldn't tell you why. But all night there
had been that roar and crash and thunder of
wind and water, and the beating of the rain on
the window pane, and every now and then the
shaking of the cabin and that cracking sound—
sometimes fairly near and again very faint,—
and I was *so* thankful that Mr. Goss had made
the men cut that tree down—the big Douglas
fir, I mean. I am sure it would have crashed

[229]

in on my cabin last night. *Would n't* you think trees two hundred feet high would have more than six or eight feet of shallow, spreading roots?

But to go back, as I began to put on my high shoes, just a minute after a hard shake of the cabin, I noticed a little damp spot on the north side. By the time I had brushed my hair and was really dressed, I just happened to look again, and, it was much larger. I opened the door and the roar of the water was enough to frighten one out of their senses, and the water seemed to be all around the cabin. But the wind had died down. I walked right into the water and around the corner—and sure enough, there was a regular stream of water coming down the trail from the pond above, and dashing right against my cabin. I could n't see why because the creek did n't seem to have overflowed, in spite of the fir tree that fell against the bridge. I got a spade out, and went up above the house and set to work to see if I could dig a trench that would divert the water. That seemed to be the only thing to do. The stream was n't so very big or strong, yet, but I did n't know what it might grow to be, and I did n't want my cabin washed away.

Well, I dug and I dug and I *dug!* And nothing I could do seemed to make any impression. If I 'd been a man, as I looked at that dancing water, swirling around my ankles, I 'd have said—*"Pshaw!"* Being a woman I *did n't.* I looked pensive and murmured "Oh, *sugar!"*

But joking aside, here I was, twenty miles from anybody—even the squatter, I guess— with floods all around me, fallen trees, as I well knew after that wind, barring the trail to Illahee, and my house in danger of being washed away—and nobody to rescue me. And yet, in spite of all that danger, I remembered a funny picture in "Life" about being "up in arms against a man"—and that was *exactly* where I longed to be. But me for the spade.

Well, I worked hours and hours, and it seemed like weeks, and suddenly a voice said, "Good heavens!" I was n't even sure I heard it. I thought I must be losing my senses. And then somebody caught me, or my arm—caught hold of me somewhere—and said, "Go right into your cabin—I 'll look after this." But I did n't go—I could n't. I was "up in arms" for a minute, and I did n't care a rap *who* the man was—though I thought I knew. Then I began to cry. I guess I 'm weak-minded, all right. But he got me into the cabin, and put a few chips on the fire—it was nearly out—and said very abruptly, "Change your clothes at once— and make me some coffee!" That brought me to. I remembered afterwards that I had n't had any breakfast.

I started the kitchen stove right away and put on the kettle and put some logs on the fire-place—I was so wet and cold—and changed into my short khaki skirt and put on my slip-pers—and then the coffee was ready. I opened the north window and called to him to come in —it was Mr. Goss, I forgot to say—but he would n't come. He made me hand the coffee out of the window to him—just two big cups-ful and went on digging with a kind of set look in his face. It seemed to me that the stream was bigger and I know the wet spot inside was wetter. I don't know how long he worked—we lost all track of time, but every once in a while I would give him a big cup of hot coffee, and by and by I saw he had got a trench so that the water ran off sidewise and down past the end of the cabin. But my whole floor was wet by that time. Then I *made* him come in and get something to eat. And do you know, it was after three o'clock! His face looked so set and stern and he was so silent, I could n't make anything out of him.

After he got something to eat and a little warmed up, he took the ax and went upstream. He said some tree must have fallen in farther up stream and diverted the water of the creek from the channel. He was gone about two hours, and when he came back he was wet and tired and as white as a ghost. It was a small tree that had been washed out by the water and a lot of bushes and they had caught in such a way as to force the water out of the creek. There's hardly any water coming down over the land now. Then he went out to look at the tree bridge and the big fir that had fallen against it. If any more trees come down there's going to be a regular jam right at the cabin and then there *will* be a flood!

But it was too late and too dark to do anything

there. I went out with him, against his will, and held the lantern for him. The bridge looks safe, though it's jarred considerably.

Then we went back to the cabin, and I cooked him another meal, and we had a roaring fire at the fireplace,—but he was so silent! I wondered then where he had dropped from. But right after supper—he wouldn't talk at all—he told me to put the lantern in good condition and if anything went wrong in the night, to wrap a piece of red cloth around it, and set it in the window. Then he would come right over. He asked for the key to the Widdy's cabin, and started off. But just before he went out of the door, he said, "Well, little girl, I guess you're safe for to-night anyway. But if anything does go wrong, remember the lantern." And then he was gone. I promise you I watched him while he climbed over the tree bridge, with that other tree resting on it. When he got to the Widdy's cabin he waved his lantern that everything was all right and then I went in.

And that was the way we spent our Christmas Day. Oh, I forgot one thing. I had hung up my stocking on the chimney the night before, and last night at supper I noticed him staring with a puzzled expression at something in the corner of the chimney, and—there was my old stocking! I jumped for it and then he laughed —not very much, but a little chuckling laugh. And every time he looked at the chimney corner, he laughed again.

The next day, he tackled that tree on the bridge. It was a dangerous piece of work, I should think, from the care with which he chopped, and the set expression of his face. But he said it had to be cut or the spring floods would surely be "disastrous." I don't know whether he meant to me or the bridge. It took him all day. The upper part of the tree had caught on the bridge, and he had to chop off the branches, and then chop off the end of the tree, and when the end fell into the stream with a splash and the water flew high, the bridge jarred and shook until I thought it would go and take him with it. But he sprang back onto the bank, and the bridge did n't go down. It slants, awfully, though. Then the trunk of the tree, without its top, was in the water, but the roots were on the land—great shallow, spreading roots, no protection at all to a tree. So he cut the tree again, about ten feet above the roots, and when that broke loose, it went floating down stream twisting and turning in the tumbling waters, and I *hope* it went over the falls. The old roots are still on the bank. That took all day.

I spent all my time that day, when I was n't out watching him, cooking—and I gave him three good meals. And he appreciated them, too. That second evening he quite thawed out, and sometimes he paced up and down the cabin, and sometimes he 'd stand in front of the fireplace and look down at me—he has wonderfully pleasant eyes. He does n't need to talk much— his eyes do it for him,—and we talked about everything in creation. I did, that is; he listened. Really, he 's the nicest man. Oh, that does n't express it. He 's quiet, really silent, but some way you feel his strength and his ability.

Well, the next day, he took the ax and went upstream. The creek was higher than ever, but the warm wind had ceased blowing alto-

gether and there was a distinct chill in the air.
I think it'll get colder now. But everything
is wet and drenched and I wanted to go with
him. At first he said no, and then when I said
how much I was shut up in the cabin,—and perhaps it might snow again—he said, oh, yes.
Come with him. He would be glad to have me.
And there was the strangest look in his eyes—
as though he was sorry for me! Sorry about
what? And when he helped me over some of
the old logs and bumpy places, he helped me
with such real gentleness, as though he were
still sorry for me. That's the only meaning I
can read into it; and I can't understand him a
bit. He cleared out a lot of snags and bushes
from the upper creek and he complimented me
on my trail-making too. Said I had done a
good piece of work. And tonight we sat here
and talked as if we were the oldest friends and
had known each other all our lives. I think
it's so strange I ever felt afraid of him. He's
gone over to the Widdy's now and it's high time
I went to bed but to-morrow he's going down to
Illahee and I wanted to send the letters with
him.

When I tried to tell him how grateful I felt, he just smiled and said something I did n't catch. But he 's been so good to me. And you know, Hope, a woman is n't very attractive when she 's in a wet gym suit, standing ankle deep in water, digging a trench, and thinking—er— thinking short, explosive thoughts. And even since then—well, when I went upstream with him to-day in my gym suit, I think I looked like a warmed-over icicle. I 've lost all sense of propriety. I 'd have gone upstream in trousers, overalls, or a harem skirt—though I 'd have preferred the trousers to the harem—but anything, *anything* except regulation skirts in a forest like this.

I tried to make him tell me to-night where he dropped from. All I could find out was that he 'd been clear up in the upper end of the district—or perhaps the next—he would n't tell much—and found a sick miner there, so he stayed and took care of him for a while, and then had to look after some sheep matters, or some measurements for sheep ranchers next spring, and so got caught by the snow and then the Chinook. He was clear off somewhere—

twenty miles away, perhaps, because the flooding of the streams forced him to make so many detours, when he decided to come over here. I wonder if that blessed man came that twenty miles just to look after the Widdy and myself! He said something about all the homesteaders being under his care—and merely a case of duty. But we got so well acquainted! And it was lots of fun cooking for him for the three days he has been here—he ate as if he was starved. It was almost like housekeeping— with one boarder—and I am glad I revived my cooking knowledge. I used all my nice china for him, too. He must get terribly tired of ironstone and enameled ware.

That's all this time. But I don't want any more experiences of that nature. Excitement is all right, but next time give me a different type, *please*. This is a long yarn, but I've nothing to do but write letters.

Affectionately,

JANE.

P. S. I wonder if Jack Burnham would ride twenty miles in flood and rain and wind to see if we were all right. I wish I hadn't looked so badly. Well, if I looked like a stewed icicle, he looked like a clothes brush. He had n't shaved for a week, and with his rough trousers tucked in boots, and flannel shirt with black tie—well, as he dug that trench and chopped those trees, he did n't look like a society man. So he need n't criticise my appearance. I wonder why that girl jilted him—the one, I mean, that I think must have jilted him. I did find out that he 's a graduate of a forestry school and has a sister who likes society and does n't like the forests and he just loves the open, and so they don't understand each other. Also he has been abroad for one summer—studying the forests of Germany.

P. S. 2. Oh, yes, I almost forgot to tell you that he stacked up my wood pile clear to the ceiling and filled every particle of space with chips and small bits of wood that would do to start a fire. Why, my cabin looks like a woodshed! But he seemed to like doing it, and I thought perhaps he wanted some excuse to stay until he was sure the flood was really over, so I did n't object. But it was not necessary.

And he asked me about a dozen times if I had plenty of matches. I wonder why.

Well, I 'm going to bed now.

J. M.

With all her perception, Jane Myers had failed lamentably in discovering several things about the strong, quiet man who had saved her so opportunely. Goss made light of the danger, though admitting that many more trees in the creek bed would have made serious trouble, but he gave her no inkling of the journey he himself had made to assure himself of her safety. Thirty miles away he had been, not twenty, owing to the rise of the mountain torrents; and the fallen trees and snow had made every foot of it a source of danger. By a straight line it was only ten miles—but the bridgeless Illahee river flowed between. He had not told her that. So thirty miles the weary horse had carried him to the cabin to find a white-faced girl struggling with woman's slight strength against the rising flood of waters which threatened the foundations of her cabin.

And another part of the story Jane could not write because the letters were in his pocket when it happened.

It was just as he was leaving. Colder weather had set in and the air was raw and frosty. There would be no new thaw until spring came. Dick, saddled and bridled, was tied to a tree near by, when Goss stopped to say good-by. There swept over him as there did at that moment over Jane, a sudden sense of the desolation of the forest in winter—of the loneliness and danger of homesteading.

"My dear little girl," he said suddenly, as he bent over her and grasped both her hands in his, "why in the world are you out here homesteading?"

And Jane, with pink cheeks, had answered, "Why, because—"

"That's a woman's reason. Because—why?"

"Why—because—"

Why had she come? Every reason she ever had vanished from mind. Every argument which had flattened out Bert Fairfax's objections, every one she had ever written to her friends, or used in moments of doubt upon herself—every one of them vanished. *"Because —"* was the only one left.

Those searching gray eyes confused her.

"Oh, it's going to be all right, now," she said after that embarrassing moment, with forced gayety. "You see it's the first of January almost, and that means that the winter is practically over. I always count spring as beginning with the first of January."

"It does begin about the first or middle of February on Puget Sound or along the coast— at Seattle, for instance,—but not here in the mountains."

"But spring will be here by the first of March, anyway. That's only two months. I shall check off every day on the calendar—you'll see when you come again."

"But I may not be up here again for a month or six weeks. I may have to go to the city for a while. And you—why you have all winter before you! But anyway, you have plenty of wood. Use it rather sparingly in mild weather, Miss Myers."

"Yes, of course,—but spring—"

"And you have plenty of matches?" he asked for the tenth time.

"Oh, yes; plenty. And spring will soon be here."

"I hope so." He spoke so gravely. And still that searching look into her face! But the thing which puzzled Jane was not the kindness of the eyes, but the pity in them. The interpretation came to her later.

And then he was off, with Dick cantering down the slope, and the rush and roar of the creek drowning out anything he might call back. But he didn't call. He only turned in his saddle as he came under the tall trees and waved his hand to her, while his experienced eyes took in, at a glance, the beauty and danger of the cabin among the tall fir trees amid the snows, its single occupant's only companions the wild beasts of the forest.

CHAPTER XV

THE TERROR OF THE FOREST

Letter from Jane Myers to Hope Denham.

February 10.

Dear Hope:

I thought I fully realized after the flood the difference between camping out in the woods for fun in summer and taking up a homestead. But the information is being rubbed in.

I 'm all alone again. The Widdy has gone to Illahee because Sammy has something or other. I don't believe there is any chance of another flood, but whatever happens this time, I guess I will need to sink or swim alone because I know both Mr. Goss and Mr. Burnham are on the Sound—and that 's a hundred miles or more away. I don't know just how far it is by the railroad. I 've hardly stepped out of my cabin since I was so frightened by that cougar. The Widdy is n't a bit of company. Besides being so superstitious, she seldom invites me

[245]

over there and never wants to come over and take a meal with me and she goes into the town so often to look after her grandchildren or her daughter that really she is n't a bit of company.

This time her son-in-law, Pat, came over here as they started off, and asked me if I wanted to go in. It meant staying in that stuffy little hotel, but still I said, "yes." But how was I to go? Pat told me to put on my snowshoes. He had his on. The Widdy rode the pony and the pony had snowshoes on. Dempsey looked so odd. But when I started for mine, I remembered one had been left under the snow, in my fright, and the straps of the other were cut— but then one would n't do any good. Pat said, "Stay here, then. I can't wait for ye." He is so rough. I don't wonder his mother-in-law prefers living alone on a homestead in the woods. So off they went—and that was some ten days ago.

I 'm afraid to go out of doors. I get water now from the snow which heaps up in that funny little extension that everybody laughed at, but it 's worth everything to me this winter. If any wild animal did spring at me, the screen would give me a chance to get into the cabin again.

But it is lonely here. The snow has banked up my north window entirely. I closed the shutter to keep out that cold, greenish pile of white. On the south side the snow has come up above the lower level of the sill. I imagine that one could walk right onto my roof from the ground at the north side and not know they had left solid earth. But you can imagine it is hard for me to amuse myself. I have nearly worn out my cookbook for ordinary dishes and when I want to make anything unusual as an experiment I find I lack some ingredient. But I am cooking as much as I can and making believe I will be rescued again though I should prefer not to repeat that experience. I can't do embroidery because the light is so dim; I have read until I am tired, and I have mended all my clothes—first time in my life such a thing ever happened—and besides all that, I made myself a new flannel shirtwaist. I usually sit between the fireplace and the window. On the other side of the fireplace is my wood. I am so glad Mr. Goss filled up everything with wood for I don't know what would happen if I should run out of it. I let both fires go out every night so as to save as much as I can, but it does take a lot of matches. However, I have two boxes left and that will carry me through I am sure —two of these big boxes of parlor matches, I mean.

So for lack of anything else to do, I decided to write something. First I tried poetry but the muse did n't seem to respond. I was working away at the poetry when this conundrum came into my head: What is the difference between a shoemaker and a poet? Do you know the answer: one makes shoes and the other shakes the muse.

I 've given up the idea of poetry. Then I tried a story. It is just started, but the characters will not do what I want them to. They are about as stubborn as if they were real people. Perhaps I shall try a bit of biography. The difficulty there is in saying true things about people. If you write it after they are dead, then it 's biography; if they 're still alive, it is slander; but if you say it on the front porch, then it 's gossip. So I guess I 'll stick to my story.

Do you know anything about copyrighting? What do you do when you copyright a story? Just what do you copyright, I mean? Is it the title, or the story, or the people and things in the story? For instance, suppose Jonah had written that story about himself and the whale —autobiography, you understand—and had copyrighted it. Would his copyright have covered the whale? Not literally, I mean, but could anybody else have written a story about that very same whale? Or would it have copyrighted Jonah himself, or just his name? Could anybody have written about Jonah if he had copyrighted himself? I'm all mixed up about it. Of course, in writing my story I wouldn't want to infringe anybody else's patent. So I'm thinking that over.

Another thing I thought of was one of those prize stories on something very moral—like "Books which have influenced me most." The "Ladies Home Journal" must pay out bushels of money for that sort of thing—and I think my ideas are as good as anybody else's. But this evening since I got to thinking over the influence of certain books on my life—Shakespeare, the Bible, Browning, because I'd have to include those three anyway,—and then Carlyle! I ought to mention him and Gibbon in order to make any sort of a showing, and Louise Alcott— it suddenly dawned on me that the one book which had most influenced me was my check book. Of course! Why am I out here in the wilderness, facing floods, and tall, gray-eyed men who looked at me pityingly—and chumming with black-eyed ones who quote poetry to me—though there's only one of each, of course, —and why am I having to write an article for the "Ladies Home Journal" in order to amuse myself if it was n't because of my check book? Check book made me teach—and you, too,— and neither Shakespeare nor Browning could influence either of us to that extent. But of course it's all up with the prize story. They'd never accept anything so mercenary as that. No; that would be a waste of time.

So I believe the story—I think I must be nervous to-night. I seem to be as hard to compose as a good comic opera. For the last hour I have heard off and on—something—I don't know what. When I listen there is nothing but the steady *tick, tick, tick,* of the clock and the light crackling of the fire. The snow and ice have dulled the roar of the creek, yet every now and then there's a queer sound—somewhere—outside.

But about my story. This is my plot. The author of my story—not myself, because it's about an author—is publishing it, serially, and the public object to a certain character because he is too rough, even for a diamond in the rough which is what he is supposed to be. (There's that queer little sound again. What can it be? Just nerves, perhaps. I think it must be the fire.) So the author takes him out of a later chapter long enough to polish him up a bit, and then the public does not like him because he is not true to his own character. They say he has lost his original force and demand the old rough char—

Through the stillness of the night came a wild, unearthly shriek. Jane's spring almost overturned the lamp. The box of matches setting on the table went flying on to the hearthstones. The girl's heart stood still. All the blood in her body was around her heart, congealing there. The cry had been so close!

Again came the fearful scream, half human yet wholly unearthly. It seemed to come from the fireplace,—or the roof. Stepping on the matches lying on the hearthstone she glanced fearfully toward the rafters, hung with bacon, ham, potatoes, lard pails, and unused kitchen utensils. Some animal must have crept in when she left her cabin door open, as she sometimes did. Remembering the fear of wild animals of fire, she threw on two fresh logs of dry wood. They snapped and crackled. Outside in the thick black forest the snow was falling silently. Inside, the fresh flames threw glancing lights and shadows into the far corners of the cabin. They gleamed and flickered on the tin dish pan in the kitchen corner and the tin pie plates ranged on a plate rail half way up the wall. In the increasing heat the matches blazed, spluttered and flickered out, or burned up. Jane paid no attention to them. Her eyes were rivetted on the dark corners of the beams, expecting to see the crouching figure of some wild animal.

Again came that wild, half-human scream, this time nearer and clearer. Not three feet away it sounded—and with nothing in between.

There was a slight scratching on the roof—then a harder scratching. Terrified by that awful cry, the faint scratching in the tense silence sickened her. From some recess in her memory there came an echo back to her:

"That tree's no more likely to fall on my cabin than a cougar is to rip off the shakes and drop in some night when I'm not expecting callers."

And the half-indifferent reply:

"That might happen, too."

Had he meant it? What sort of claws did a cougar have? Jane tried to think. Again the light scratching. The cougar had come close to the warm chimney and was burrowing through the snow to the roof. *Could* a cougar rip off the shakes and get down into the cabin?

The chimney was large, but there was little fear of the animal's using the chimney route because of the fire. The thought of firearms did not occur to her.

She sank back in a chair, weak and faint.

[253]

She was there alone. Absolutely alone in that wild, lonely forest of the Illahee. Her cabin might burn, some cougar break through the roof, or the wolves attack her, if they got a chance, and not a soul in all the world would know of it. No one would be there to protect her, and with the thought of protection came the memory of Goss's face as he asked about the wood pile,—the serious, thoughtful face with the kind look in the gray eyes. Yes, he knew it. She suddenly understood. *He* must have met the Terror of the Forest. That was why he had looked at her pityingly. And if he were there, it would be all right, of course. No cougar would dare attack her if a man were there. It was because she was a woman and alone. If any one would come—anybody! Just as Leonard Goss had come that day of the floods. If a cougar should break through the roof, what should she do?

Again the memory of Goss brought back vague commands. Never leave your cabin without firearms—that was one thing he had said. Of course! She had forgotten them. With shaking knees she walked across the room, stepping on two or three matches and noting their light flicker as she picked up the revolver. The wild yell came from above again. The revolver dropped from nerveless fingers. Then grasping it, she returned to the fireplace. Two more logs of wood went into the blaze. She would meet the danger with fire and with fire-arms. No cougar should eat her without some risk.

For hours she sat there, waiting, listening, every muscle tense and every nerve strained—listening—listening, for the fall of a heavy body through the roof, or even down the big cat-and-clay chimney.

Again and again through the peace of the night came that ghastly scream. Jane heard it with chattering teeth and blood that ran cold. Now and then, in the heat, the sputter of a match caught her attention. She only watched to see they did not set fire to anything. There was little danger, though. They were on the hearthstone.

Goss's face came back to her as he had grasped her hands that morning when he left, after he had saved her from the flood. "My

dear little girl—" What *was* it he had said
about matches. A vague fear, aside from the
cougar, came into her mind.

"Are you sure you have enough matches?"
That was what he had said. Yes, she had
plenty. There was a box on the table and another box on the mantle. She had more than
she needed. She had given the Widdy a full
box just a day or two before she started for Illahee. But the thought of matches came back.

"Are you sure you have enough matches?"
She could hear Goss say the words. She could
see the pity in his eyes as he stood there and
looked down upon her. "My dear little girl—"
She looked at the match box on the table—but
it was not there. She must have set it to one
side. Listlessly she looked at the tiny charred
sticks lying around in front of the fire. Those
had been matches. Thought began to come
back to her. And there was the empty box—on
the floor. With a sudden spring, as the realiza-
tion of the truth came over her, she began to
search the hot stones for unburned matches.
The fire scorched her face, the hot bricks
burned her skirt, yet she could find but two

[256]

good matches. But there was the other box on the mantle. Confidently, yet fearfully, she looked into it. There were four matches in the bottom—four puny little sticks. She had but six matches, and perhaps most of the winter still before her!

Only twice more in the darkness did the cougar scream, yet each scream seemed nearer, a triumphant, exulting note, to the terrified girl in the cabin.

It was broad daylight in the outer world, the world of spruce boughs swaying under their weight of snow, the world of frozen streams and snow-blanketed forests, before Jane dared relax her vigilance sufficiently to lie down for a little sleep. Even then it was a broken sleep, though the tightly barred room was as dark as night. No letting of fires out now. Those six matches might have to do for months yet. Perhaps for centuries. It would be centuries, of course, before all that snow melted.

It was ten o'clock when Jane, aroused by a slight flicker in the dying fire, sprang to her feet certain that the cougar had come down the chimney and was in the cabin. Ten o'clock but with both windows and the door barred, it might have as well been midnight. The animal was not there as she reassured herself as clearer thought came to her, because if it were, very likely she would not be—at any rate not whole and sound.

Carefully she stirred the dying embers until a faint flicker rewarded her. Matches were to be saved for absolute necessity, and cooking must be done now before the open fire to save fuel.

When the blaze was crackling merrily, and her fears somewhat comforted by its cheerful radiance, she went to the south window. The north one for days she had not opened, as she had written Hope. It had snowed during the night but little, yet the snow lay piled up two inches above the sill. It was clear and sunny outside, and she could see the snowy crests of the forest trees against the keen blue of the winter sky. The world was very beautiful outside, yet dangerous, too, for there fell upon her ear the distant, long-drawn cry of a wolf. Answering cries seemed nearer, and sick again at heart the girl turned to her fire. Absolutely alone, in that terrible forest,—for it was no longer beauti-

ful. The Terror of the Forest was upon her—
the horror of it all.

Well enough Jane knew the meaning of the
long-drawn howl of the wolf calling to the pack.
The deep snow had driven the deer down to the
lower levels and even now some deer leaping
and bounding and plunging through the snow
was being trailed by the sharp-fanged, gaunt
timber-wolves.

The nights were full of horror after that, for
the cougar's scream came often through the
darkness. Nor were the days much better with
the far cries of the wolves in full chase after
some helpless deer. Only to have known that
the Widdy was in the cabin across the creek
would have been an immense relief, even though
with cougars, wolves, and the ice and snow,
neither could have reached the other. But to
be alone!

Evening after evening as she sat before the
fire, her mind went back to the days Goss had
spent with her during the flood. Again and
again as she looked up, he seemed to be standing
before the fireplace looking down at her with
that expression of pity in his eyes. She under-

[259]

stood now—understood altogether too well! He had urged her, as strongly as he could, to come into town for the winter months, but remembering the hotel there, her only place of refuge, she had refused. She had been so certain that spring would come early. It always did in the Northwest! Then when he had suggested that she go to her friends at Spokane at least until the middle of March, she had answered proudly that she came out to take up a homestead and to live in it, not to run away during the most beautiful months of the year. And he had admitted that the winter was beautiful—but dangerous, too. She had been so sure of herself! And now!

Jane realized that her only salvation lay in keeping herself busy. She cooked diligently, even trying entirely new dishes; but everything tasted flat. She tried to read serious books—books deliberately saved for the stormy days of winter because demanding thought and concentration. She could not get the meaning of a single paragraph through her head.

She picked up an unopened paper one afternoon with a sense of surprise. It had slipped behind the table and lain there unnoticed. The very surprise aroused her, and she was deeply interested in it when a sudden shadow falling on the square of sunlight at her feet made her look up. With his nose close to the window pane, licking his jaws, stood a huge gray timber-wolf. Behind him, looking in, stood two others. A single leap would have brought all three through the frail sash into the cabin itself. For a moment Jane was frozen to her chair; then with a sudden motion threw the paper toward the fireplace. It was too feeble a throw, and only the edge touched the wood. Would it burn? Dare she move? The wolves licked their jaws. Then a sudden blaze as the paper caught, burning out on the hearth, and the three gaunt figures stepped back in fear of the Red Flower of the Forest! It was her one chance. With a spring the girl caught the heavy inside shutter and flung it to, barring it with hands that shook as she expected every moment to feel flung against it the weight of the forest robbers. It was fastened at last—after ages of fumbling,—and as the blaze of the burning paper died away the plucky girl sank into the nearest chair.

How long after that it was, Jane never knew. She had lost all track of time, and seldom knew whether it was night or day in the dark, closely-barred cabin. Centuries it seemed; and at times, as she heard the familiar shriek of the cougar and the near cry of the wolf pack she wondered whether her hair were growing white. For the oil was very low in the can, there were but four matches now, and the wood pile, too, was lessening. The world outside was a blank to her.

So she never knew that the snow had ceased, that a light warm wind had begun the spring thaw, and that flood time was near again.

It was years and years after Pat and Mrs. Patton had gone into Illahee that Jane thought she heard one morning the old, familiar yodel down the trail. But it could not be. It was simply that she was losing her mind. Think of all the times that cougar had been right there in her cabin, lashing his tail, just ready to spring upon her when she forced herself to see there was no animal there. And Goss! Night after night he had stood there in the corner of the fireplace looking down upon her, always with

[262]

that concerned, pitying look in his eyes, only of late there was a deepening of the pity. He had come to tell her there was no escape; that if her matches or her wood gave out, she would freeze to death and there was no one to save her. The yodel was all a part of the horror of it.

Yet nearer and clearer it sounded—nearer and nearer—and there was some one pounding on the door, and calling to her—calling—calling—

It must be hallucination—it might be wolves flinging themselves against the barred door—but slowly, slowly the girl's shaking hands unbarred it. The door flew open as a mass of snow fell into the room under the feet of two men—and one of them suddenly jumped and caught her—

The second man went straight to the mantle and looked at the four matches in the box; then at the half dozen pieces of wood in the corner. "Good heavens!" was all he said.

CHAPTER XVI

THE SQUATTER

THE far, faint scream of a cougar one sunny May morning sent Jane flying into her cabin, panic-stricken. It was a very faint, distant sound, and had it not been for her experience of the winter she might not have heard it at all. But she listened, tense and rigid, at the window for a clearer and nearer repetition of the cry. It did not come and she began to reason with herself.

"A cougar is a coward, Jane. You know that. They'd never touch a grown person in broad daylight, and in the spring, too, when there are plenty of young fawns."

The May sunshine was alluring, the washtub was emphatic, and Jane at last ventured into the fresh, soft air, and began her work. Yet she was alert for any stealthy or unusual sound which might reach her over the rush of the creek

[264]

as it swirled down to go thundering over the falls. The cry had not come from the other side of the creek. That occurred to her as she listened intently. The cougar seemed to keep entirely on her side of the stream.

She began her washing, still alert though there was little chance that any sound from a cougar's padded feet would reach her, and a near-by warning scream would have frozen her to the spot. But with all her listening she did not hear the tread of a horse coming up the trail until a whinny close to her made her jump a foot.

"I did n't mean to startle you, 'pon honor." Burnham's jolly laugh was infectious. "You seemed to be listening and I thought you heard me."

"I was listening. I heard—I thought—I mean—" She paused in confusion. She was beginning to fear these men would regard her as a coward.

"What did you think you heard?"

"A few minutes ago I heard a cougar scream. It was far away. I heard just the faintest sound,—but it was a cougar. And just as you

[265]

came up I thought I heard something beyond that log. It must have been Bob."

"Do you remember telling me of that ravine Sam fell into last fall?" Burnham sat on his horse and looked beyond the big fir into the green depths beyond. "I believe that these cougars of yours must have their lair in that sheltered hollow. It's an ideal place for them, or for bears."

"Oh, do you think there is more than one?" There was genuine alarm in her tone.

"Oh, no. How large is that ravine?"

"I measured it with a long pole and it was certainly over twenty feet deep in that spot. Is it really a hidden ravine?"

"Probably. That's nothing unusual. The trees fall and others fall over them. In the decaying punk bushes take root. It's not unusual."

"I don't like the idea of a cougar's lair on my homestead. There isn't room for both of us."

"A cougar skin would make a good rug for you. But I haven't any trap with me."

"I haven't, either. I never dreamed of needing such a thing."

"Let me see if the Widdy has one. She ought to be up on woodcraft."

He sprang off his horse and crossed the narrow bridge. It was some time before he reappeared, and Jane, her washing deserted, began to pat Bob. Again the slight sound from the tangle caught her ear. She looked apprehensively at the prostrate fir and the forest beyond, but there was nothing. With Burnham near, her fears had slight hold and she forgot it as he came triumphantly, holding a steel spring trap from which dangled a heavy chain.

"Want to come with me? Let's see if we can catch Mr. Cougar."

To venture right into his lair!

She stepped into the house and picked up her revolver. It was the first time she had been any distance into the forest since spring had come. Her trail work had been along the creek toward the lake. She had almost forgotten cougars until the scream of the morning brought back the winter's fears.

Over the invisible trail which the two woodsmen seemed to see so easily they passed, Jane close at the trapper's heels; then striking off

[267]

before they crossed the hidden ravine, Burnham paused at a spot where it ended in a mere depression of the ground, lightly wooded with young alders and a few scrub firs. They were hardly beginning to leaf out yet. Fastening the heavy chain to one end of a heavy log, Burnham baited the trap, after setting it in a likely place near the cougar's trail, and rejoined Jane who had stood at some distance expecting every moment to feel the blow from a springing animal.

"If Goss comes up here before I get back," he said, as they struck out for the cabin again, "tell him about this trap, will you? We want to kill that brute and have done with him. I hadn't thought of this ravine as his camping place before."

Burnham regained his horse and Jane her washtub. He mounted and paused for a moment.

"I came up a moment to see if you were all right, on my way to Illahee. I'll be back again in a few days. Shall I bring up your mail? Goss may possibly come down before I get here, but it's hardly likely. Several of the rangers are to meet up the valley next week, to make plans for fire fighting. The supervisor is to be here. I don't believe he'll have time to come down. Good-by!"

Jane turned to the interrupted washing. Saturday should not be washday in a properly constituted household, but such theories fade out in forest life. She was trying to bake, too. "No more winter," she thought as she picked out some handkerchiefs, "no more snow, no more floods, no more cougars, no more—*squatters,*" she was going to add when a slight rustle made her turn quickly to find herself facing the squatter again.

"What do you want?" she demanded in a reasonably firm tone. Burnham's presence had left her with more courage.

"Sumthin' ter eat." The voice was hardly more than a growl.

Controlling herself, she studied the fragment of human wreckage which stood before her. Gaunt, emaciated, dirty, with tatters flying in the light May breeze, ragged holes in elbows and knees, shifting eyes and furtive air,—could one call him a man, she wondered? Yet the

[269]

sight of the human suffering took away every vestige of fear.

"Go sit down near the trunk of that tree," she said quietly, "and I will get you something to eat."

He looked at her without moving.

"Did you hear what I said?" She repeated it in a louder voice, with forefinger pointing to a place some hundred feet from the cabin door.

The squatter shuffled slowly away toward the fir.

Jane went into her kitchen, belted on her revolver, and barred the door. She did not feel the slightest fear of the man now, yet she did not care to turn around and find him at the door. It was with a sense of pity for human misery that she picked up the steaming kettle and made the coffeepot full of strong coffee. It was only a few minutes before ham was sizzling on the hot stove, and when all was done, she loaded a tray with a pitcher of coffee, steaming hot, sugar, canned cream, ham and eggs, bread and butter. She could not have set a much better impromptu meal before Burnham himself. Unfastening the door she looked out. The squatter sat on the log, watching the cabin. There was a quick movement of his head as she came out, a half effort to rise, and then he waited until she walked half way toward him and set the tray on the stump of a small tree, motioning him to come there.

With revolver still in her belt, she resumed her work at the tub, watching the derelict out of the corners of her eyes. She had never seen a starving man eat before, and she never wanted to again. The ferocity with which he attacked the food made her shudder, even while it deepened the ache in her heart. In social settlement work she might have become accustomed to the men of the bread line, but her teaching had not brought her in contact with that side of life. Watching him, she began to speculate.

Suppose he was a murderer? Suppose he had committed some other crime? She would give him food, even though it were a crime in itself. That was clear. She would never refuse food to any starving man, but suppose she were helping to defeat the ends of justice? He was a fugitive. That was unquestioned. What were the ends of justice? Justice would arrest him, put him in jail, perhaps hang him. But its object would be punishment, and at the thought of punishment her hazy moral sense cleared up. Nothing she could do would defeat the ends of justice for he was punishing himself as no court would ever do. She looked again at the tattered wreck. He had almost emptied the tray. Then she walked over to him.

"If you will wait a little while," she said in a kindly voice, "I will give you some food to take with you." He looked up at her without a word. The light striking on his face brought out painfully the hollow eyes and the fleshless cheeks.

"Stay here until I bring you more food."

She went into the cabin again, and this time she did not close the door. More ham went into the frying pan, the fragrant coffee was steaming, and the long knife was cutting the last loaf of bread when the Widdy flashed through the open door.

"What you a-feedin' that man fur?" she demanded brusquely.

"Because he is hungry."

"How 'jer know he ain't goin' to kill yer?"

"He might—if I did n't give him any food. He is almost starved, Mrs. Patton."

"An' now he 'll hang aroun' all the time. He 's been doin' it fur a year."

"I can't help it. I can't let any man, no matter how much of a criminal he may be, starve before my eyes. I 'm glad you 've come over, though. I am going to wrap this up for him to take away. And I 'm going to give him more coffee. It 's strong, too."

Jane wrapped up the bundle of food as she talked and picking up the coffeepot she started again for the fugitive. She refilled the pitcher from the pot in her hand. Hot and strong, he drank it down eagerly. His capacity seemed unlimited.

"Tell me who you are," she said.

No answer but a stare.

"Tell me what your name is and where you live."

Still no answer, but the shifty eyes were watching her closely. She felt a sudden sense of repulsion.

"This is more food for you," she said, handing him the package. "Don't eat it now.

Wait until to-morrow or next day. And never, *never* come on my claim again. You have no right on my homestead. Do you hear?"

She left him still staring and went back to face the condemnation and reproaches of the sharp-tongued Widdy. The squatter arose slowly and shuffled down the trail. In a moment he was lost to view.

At sundown that evening Leonard Goss came up the trail. Though the evening was chilly, the cabin door was open to let out the smell of the cooking.

"Come in," she called. "You're my third caller. I'm keeping open house to-day."

The Widdy appeared at her door and he waved to her. She vanished.

"Did you give them as cordial a welcome as you do me?" he asked, as he dropped her hand. "I suppose Burnham was one. I can't guess the other."

"Mr. Burnham was the first one. The squatter was the next."

"Is he around again?" Goss dropped down on the doorsill.

"Yes—and starving. I gave him an immense

meal. He ate it ravenously. Then I gave him more food to carry away."

Goss looked at her for a moment incredulously, and then caught sight of the revolver in her belt.

"I thought you were afraid of him."

"I was until I saw how starved and miserable he was. The Widdy says he will be back here for food all the time now. I told him he must never come on my homestead again. Do you think he will?"

"I don't know." Goss spoke slowly. "He might if he were hungry. Starvation will drive a man to almost anything, you know. If he did come again and were hungry, I should give him food,—yes. It's safer, let alone being more humane. But keep your revolver within reach."

"That was my point of view, but you should have heard the Widdy scold. Yet I don't see either, why she should have much right to scold me. All the spring,—nearly—that empty cabin of hers has been desolation itself. Really, Mr. Goss, she is not a bit of company for me."

"I know it. I have been thinking about that.

[275]

But if I don't go to supper now, I 'll be the one to get a scolding." He laughed. "I wonder how she knew I was coming."

"She thinks you and Mr. Burnham travel in pairs."

"Wish we did,—but thanks to that old cabin we do see something of each other. I 'll come over after supper. I want you to go up the valley with me to-morrow. Several of the rangers will be there with their wives."

CHAPTER XVII

UP THE VALLEY

JANE thought she was up early the next morning, but when the straight line of blue smoke from her chimney notified her neighbors that the first move had been made toward breakfast, and she opened her door to get water from the creek, she was surprised to find Goss sitting on a log near by with the tawny skin of a cougar in a heap beside him.

"Here's your friend!" he called cheerfully.

The fire in the cook stove crackled merrily for some minutes after that, without even a kettle of water to heat.

Jane looked him over carefully. Nine feet he measured from the tip of his nose to the tip of his tail, tawny yellow on the back shading down to a rabbit gray on the under part of the body. He was not a pleasant-looking beast, with long, strong claws, and sinister, malignant mouth. Even though he was dead and skinned, Jane shivered a little.

"He was caught by the right foot," explained Goss. "Did n't you hear him yowl last night?"

"I did n't hear a sound." A moment later, studying the claws, she asked the question she had wondered over many a time. "Could that cougar have ripped the shakes off my roof last winter?"

"If he actually wanted to, he probably could have done it. If he had been starving and knew there was food—and knew he could get it that way. They do attack children, fawns, young calves,—the more helpless creatures,—but they are really great cowards. If attacked and cornered, he might have fought hard—or he might not. If he were fighting for a meal, and were starved, as I said, he would probably put up a stiff fight. On the whole, they are cowardly."

The cabin door across Thunder Creek opened and the Widdy flagged the ranger. He arose at once.

"I 'll bring Dempsey over for you," he said

as he picked up the bucket. "Will you be ready in half an hour?" He brought the water to the door and set it down. Jane proceeded to hurry breakfast.

Dempsey had not been under the saddle for many a day when Goss pulled the rearing, plunging animal across the creek, while Jane looked on, aghast at the idea of riding him.

"You ride Dick," he said, as he noticed her startled face. "You couldn't manage this beast."

He shortened the stirrups on Dick for her and lengthened those on Dempsey for himself. The Widdy not only used the ordinary cross saddle of the mountains, but a man's saddle.

"All right," he called, as Dempsey started off after a preliminary flourish.

"All right," answered Jane. "Get up, Dick." Dick considered the matter. Jane flicked him with the whip. "Come," she said, picking up the reins, "get up, Dick." She gave him a sharper blow on the flank. Dick turned and looked carefully at the woman on his back. Another blow and a harder one. A few muscles twitched.

Goss looked back and seeing her motionless, rode back.

"How do you start this animal, Mr. Goss?" she asked with flushed face, mortified by Dick's theories of passive resistance. His undisguised amusement brought more color.

"Come, Dick," he called, and Dick obeyed with his usual willingness.

It was a glorious May morning. Thunder Creek as they rode beside it, flooded with the melting snows, rushed and crashed and roared, yet this morning the homesteader heard only the music of its thunder. It no longer terrified her with its threats. Winter was gone with the wet black panes, the high wind and pattering rain, the cold green light of the snowed-up windows, the howling of wolves and the screaming of cougars. Instead there was the softest of tender blue skies, a clear, warm, friendly sunshine, the light breeze rippling over the fresh green of the new growths, and the occasional song of the birds.

At the foot of Thunder Creek trail, half a mile below, they encountered a train of pack horses, loaded with tents, blankets, provisions,

[280]

and other supplies, bound for the ranger's head-quarters. The two reined in to let the train pass them, and Jane watched with delighted eyes the steady, sure-footed tread as they plunged into the icy waters of Thunder Creek. Dick followed them easily, shivering a little as he forded the stream, but Dempsey reared and snorted and plunged, and then dashed through the cold water at breakneck speed.

The girl had never been so happy in her life. At last winter was really over. She realized it more fully as they rode on. Spring had come in earnest. The dogwood trees were white with creamy, brown-centered blossoms, and the wild cherries, seen here and there along the streams, were snowy white. Cedars and spruce and firs were tipped with light green spikes of new growth. In the tiny mountain parks, which grew more numerous as they advanced, were the wild rhododendrons, fields of them, it seemed to her, with magenta-tinged purple blossoms,— the state flower of her newly adopted state. In the entangled undergrowth of the forests were wild roses, not yet in blossom, the yellow flowers of the Oregon grape, the pale green of

[281]

its soft, tender leaves differing strangely from the hard, stiff, dark green leaves of late summer with their holly-like barbs. The white, waxen blossoms of the salal gleamed from the new green leaves still adorned with light pink bracts, and the darker, glossy leaves of the older growth of this evergreen shrub. The service berry bushes were in blossom, and wild columbine, in sunny spots, while in the forests the new fronds of the sword ferns and of the fern brake gave yet another shade of green to the forest growth.

The fears of the winter were gone. Homesteading was a success. The cool mountain breeze swept the trail under the towering trees, with the ever-present fresh coolness of the Northwest, and the sunshine filtered through the cool green forest in golden patches of light. Blue sky, in tiny patches, was visible through the swaying crests so far above.

Often the trail wound, as it did nearer Illahee, under or around great fallen trees. As they turned back to the main trail, Jane noticed a fire-warning sign, somewhat different from those she had seen before:

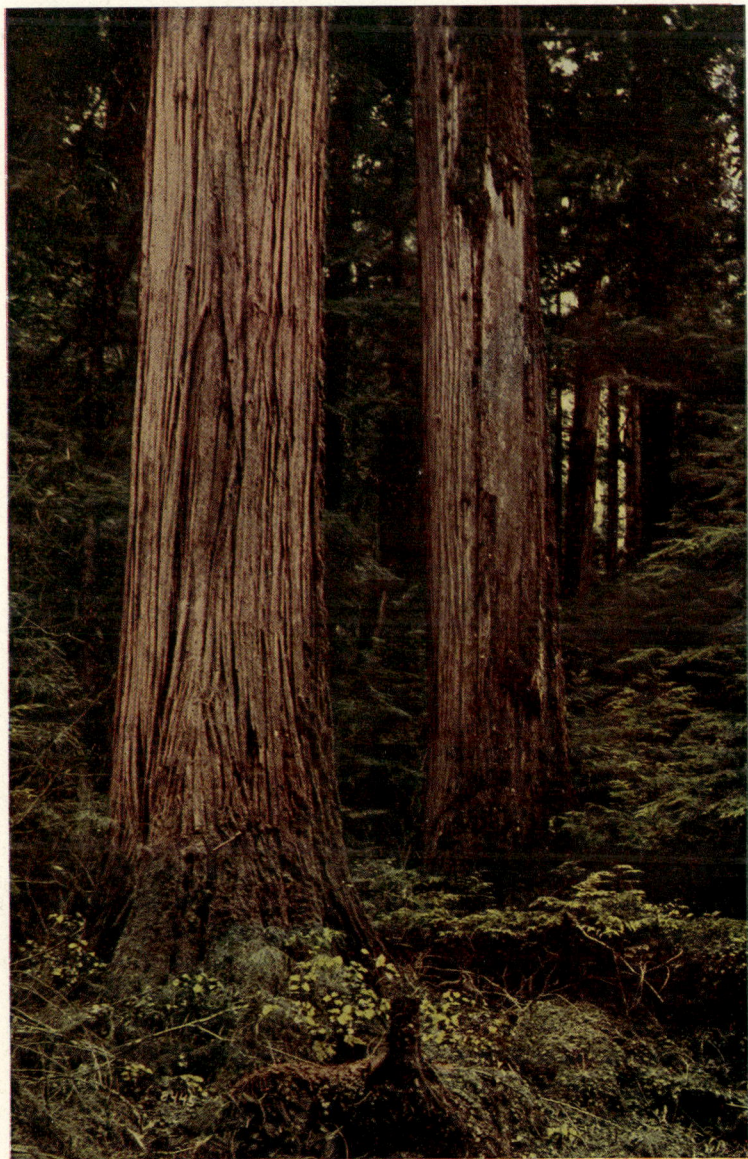

The cool green depths of a Washington forest

FOREST FIRES!
WARNING

IT IS UNLAWFUL AND PUNISHABLE BY FINE AND IMPRISONMENT,

First--To set and leave any fire that may spread to adjacent timber or other property.

Second--To burn slashings, choppings, and the like, from June 1st to October 1st, without a permit issued by a Fire Warden or Forest Ranger.

Third to operate spark-emitting locomotives, engines or boilers without using safe and effective spark arresters.

Fourth--To deface, destroy or remove this notice.

Fifth--To refuse to render assistance in suppressing timber fires when called upon by Fire Wardens or Rangers.

Sixth--Campers, prospectors, hunters, fishermen and others are warned against kindling and using fire where it is liable to spread and destroy timber or other property, and are advised to build fires, when necessary, in the beds of streams which are exposed during the dry season, or on open, clear ground. In every instance thoroughly quench your fire before leaving it. This may save you great trouble and expense.

See Chapter 164, Laws of 1905, and Chapter 125 Laws of 1911.

Approved by the
State Board of Forest Commissioners
May 13, 1911.

J. R. WELTY
STATE FORESTER AND FIRE WARDEN

E. L. BOARDMAN, PUBLIC PRINTER, OLYMPIA.

Windfalls from the previous winter had as yet been chopped away only in the worst places along the route. Five miles above Thunder

Creek, as Goss turned into a short side trail a log cabin hidden among the trees came into view.

Jane suddenly realized where she was. Two horses, saddled, stood near the door. Goss whistled, waited, then rapped on the door with his riding whip.

"Is this where my furniture landed?" she asked, remembering the hilarity with which her friends had told her of their unexpected freight yard.

Goss laughed and nodded. The occupants of the cabin were ready to join them. They were introduced as Mr. Gates and his wife. He was a ranger from the district across the river, and with his wife had used the cabin as a half-way house on their way up the valley. The four were soon on their way.

Up they climbed and then down again, as the trail wound through the forest, yet the general elevation was higher and Jane knew there must be falls in the river below. The mountains on the opposite side of the Illahee fell back from the river and lay in long folds, mile after mile and league after league, each, half revealing,

[284]

half concealing another, forest covered, blue with the soft mists which blended with the deep blue at the edge of the world, where the serene blue above met the softer tint beneath. And always, somewhere, snow glistened in the sunlight.

Here and there along the trail, where the drifts of the winter had piled deep in a hollow in the forest, there were still patches of snow into which the horses sank, plunging desperately to get a footing in the snowy depths. Trickling streams of water gurgled from the edges of such patches.

"Hold the reins loosely and give him his head," directed Goss as Dick went almost headlong into an unexpected depth of snow, kicking and struggling to get his footing. And the plucky little animal soon pulled himself out of it. They went more slowly over the snow, but Goss led with a sure knowledge of the hidden trail. Then they wound downward again, and before the middle of the morning they had reached headquarters, a two-story house of peeled and varnished logs at the foot of a mountain, dark with forests, but almost in the midst

[285]

of a long, level stretch, green with the new spring crops.

Ordinary conversation is impossible to any group of people strung out in a line, following, Indian fashion, along a narrow trail. So, though Jane got the sense of good fellowship from the two who had joined them, and knew herself dependent upon friendly Mrs. Gates as chaperone, she had little chance to become acquainted with the pleasant-faced, vigorous woman, not much older than herself.

The object of getting the rangers together was to discuss plans for united work in adjoining districts for fire fighting during the coming summer. The districts of the men were tremendous in extent. Goss, for instance, was in charge of more than two hundred thousand acres of country, densely wooded, with craggy peaks, susceptible to lightning strokes, heavily forested, with precipitous breaks in the mountain sides, impassable by reason of fallen trees and the jungle of undergrowth except as fire trails or pack trains were built through it

Mrs. Gates and Jane spent the afternoon in a long walk to various points where they were in sight of the mountains beyond the river, clothed with mysterious, shimmering blue. But her companion understood something of her husband's work, and the talk at meal times was on fire fighting, so it was not hard to learn the essentials of that all-important work. The principles were few but comprehensive; a quick arrival at the fire; an adequate force; proper equipment; thorough organization of the fighting crew; a knowledge of the country; and skill in meeting any particular fire by the quickest and most effective method of meeting its particular characteristics.

Trails were badly needed. The year before, in a district across the river, a fire had been seen from a lookout point, but it had taken three full days for the fire guards to locate it, partly because of the inaccessibility of that gulch, through density of the forest and lack of trails, and also because of the thick, all-enveloping smoke. Underneath every plan that the rangers laid could be heard the mention of fire trails. Fire breaks were also needed—stretches deliberately laid waste and bare, between sections of the forest,—but they must come when Congress made a larger appropriation. The fact that millions of dollars of valuable timber were going up in smoke every year did not seem to bring the necessary monetary resources for the needed protection of the forests.

Without trails and equipment, buried at convenient points along the trails, the men could do their best, yet it might amount to nothing. Efficiency depended upon the skill and experience of the man directing the work. He must judge as to the character of the fire as well as of the forest, the strength and direction of the wind, the condition of the atmosphere, the rapidity with which the fire was running, and the best method of attack. Small surface fires could be beaten out, as they often were, by a ranger who might find them, with long, sidewise strokes of a wet burlap, or perhaps his own coat. In a forest covered with an inflammable carpet of needles and with brushwood, dirt thrown on flames had but little effect. Iron buckets and bucket pumps were not practicable in the mountains, but special packs of tools, ready to place upon a horse's back and including collapsible pails, axes, mattocks, ropes, provisions, were kept in convenient places as well as at the ranger's headquarters.

Mrs. Gates talked much more freely of her husband's work than Goss did of his own. Jane was interested in everything. She had taken it for granted that a ranger ought to be able to do ordinary cooking,—making bread and preparing meats,—but it had not occurred to her that an intimate knowledge of locations with good grass for the horses, good water, good fishing, if possible, and, in dry seasons, such locations that fires may not burn out his outfit, were absolutely required. She learned, too, that it was obligatory upon a ranger to know as well as possible all the people within the boundaries of his district, and that his success depended upon his tact and skill in dealing with them, as well as with the sheep men who ranged their herds in the open glades. She did know, of course, for Goss had told her, that one of their duties was to protect the game, and to rid the reserves of ruthless hunters who kill for heads and horns, or for teeth only.

"And a man must be strong," said Mrs. Gates. "Any man that peters out in no time ain't got no call to come into a forest reserve."

Jane's memory went back to the Christmas floods, and the days of work that followed the long, hard ride.

"And the forest fires?"

"Thet's the worst work of all, 'specially when the fires get high and the hired workers keep 'em going for the sake of the pay."

That was a phase of fire fighting which Goss had never discussed with her. In fact, as she thought back over their talks, forest fires was the one subject which he had carefully avoided. She determined to make him tell her about it at the first opportunity.

Goss joined her after supper that night as she stood with her hands in her sweater pockets looking at the blue ridges of mountains. The sun was gradually sinking toward the highest distant peak.

"Did Mrs. Gates show you the seed dryer?" he asked.

"Seed dryer! No. What is it?"

"Come and see."

They wandered off to the tentlike structure, rather closely shelved, though exposed to the breeze on all sides, in which cones were ripened and dried until the seeds could be collected.

"I never heard you talk about picking cones!"

"I never pick them."

"I thought you said that collecting cones was part of your work."

"It is. Can you guess how?"

Jane thought a moment.

"Cones usually do not fall until they are pretty ripe, and you are likely to lose many of the seeds—even then the squirrels would get them before you did. No, I can't guess. Do you climb the trees?"

"We rob the squirrels."

"That's mean."

"No, it isn't. They can get more. You see squirrels run out on the uppermost branches, to the far tips, where the best cones grow. They nibble them off and let them fall, and then gather them around some favorable hole and hide them."

"Then you rangers steal them."

"The squirrels don't starve. We take them early in the fall when they have time to lay in another supply. It's the only way to get the

[291]

best seeds. Sometimes a single squirrel will hide two bushels of fat cones."

"Plucky little things."

"Yes, Uncle Sam's four-footed friends. The rangers send the cones to headquarters, seeds are collected and sifted, and used to reforest other districts."

They wandered away from the dryer to a rocky point to watch the sunset. The long, north country twilight was before them, and Goss had news for her—news which might mean much for both of them. Also he had a question he wanted to ask her. But there was plenty of time and she might lead up to it, unintentionally.

"This is wonderful to me," she said, as she looked over at the sweep of mountain before them, a soft gray-blue against a clear yellow light. The sun had set behind that topmost ridge. "I have been in among the trees so long! Here there is such a view—and how wonderfully beautiful it is."

They stood in silence watching the deepening of the soft blue. There was a tinge of pink in the sky now.

"I once heard some one," Jane said, as she sat down on the end of a log, "make a remark about the Land of Little Sticks. That has been in my mind all day, though they could never call this country such a name."

She looked around to the mountain rising directly above with its tall straight trees and its wilderness tangle. Drifting on the evening breeze came the reek of the camp fire, pungent yet pleasant, and the sound of men's voices in a jolly chorus.

"It's a country suggestive of romance. I don't wonder that the *voyageurs* and the fur hunters of the old fur-trading companies could not go back to civilization. This whole country, with its wonderful snow peaks, the massive mountain ridges, dense forests, and its rivers—it's all romantic. I never yet have been on the Columbia river in the evening that I did not dream I heard the echo of some old *chanson,* sung in time to the dip of the paddle."

It was romantic. The slender, graceful outlines of an Indian tepee, with a fire glimmering on the ground before it, would have carried them back, perhaps, forty or fifty years to

[293]

earliest pioneer days; or, still farther back, to the boating songs of the *voyageurs*.

"I have some news for you to-night," he said after a long silence, seating himself beside her. The mountains were darker now, but still that wonderful gray-blue, every peak and ridge outlined sharply against a background of orange and gold. The pink had faded out. "I have just received my appointment as deputy supervisor of the reserve."

"Good! Congratulations!" exclaimed Jane. She knew how much the delayed promotion meant to him. "You will be able to do more for the forests now." She looked up at him, recalling Burnham's remark, "Goss is a king among men." She agreed with him fully.

"Yes—much more. Ellison is to take my place. You met him, did n't you?" Jane remembered a man whom Mrs. Gates said was new.

"Then you knew it before?"

"I knew it must come soon. Mr. Granger knew it, so he brought up Ellison. He did n't telephone it because he said he wanted to surprise me."

[294]

"I am so glad. Tell me about your new work."

But the new deputy supervisor had other things on his mind.

"Tell me what you did to keep yourself busy last winter—when you were snowed in," he asked suddenly. "I should have thought you would have gone crazy."

"I guess I nearly did, toward the last—when the wood began to give out." She wondered why, when he had so studiously avoided that subject, he should begin to talk of it now and with such interest in his tone.

"I sewed and mended and cooked and tended the fire," she went on, "and read, or tried to, and slept—a little—and tended the fire. It always wound up with tending the fire. I cooked before the open fireplace to save wood—and pretended I was camping out—and then—"

"Then what?" He hoped she would give him some opening soon.

"I tried to write a story. But I got all tangled up over the copyright."

"What did that have to do with the story?"

He was smiling down at her now, and when

[295]

he smiled in that teasing way, Jane always felt
as though she were a very small child.

"Stories have to be copyrighted, you know."

"But not until after they are written."

"Oh!" There was a long, comprehensive
silence. "You see I never thought of trying
such a thing before, and I did n't know anything
about it."

"How did you get 'tangled'?"

"I could n't quite understand what it was that
was copyrighted—that 's why. I wanted to settle it beforehand. Suppose I had been writing
about a doodle bug or a dinky bird, and some
one else had written about them and copyrighted it—would I be infringing their patent?"

"I think not." His voice was very gentle.
"You see you might touch upon another phase
in the life of the doodle bug—"

"I don't believe I make it clear. Suppose I
wrote something about myself. If I copyrighted it, then nobody could ever write about
me except myself? Or if I wrote it and somebody else copyrighted it, would that give them
any claim on me—any hold on me?"

"I wish it did," he said under his breath. Here was his chance.

"I think I see your point," he said aloud. "Do you know what I would like to have you do? Write the story of your experiences last winter and let me copyright it. I think that would be an excellent plan."

"Would n't that give you some sort of authority over me? I never even thought about copyrighting until I decided to write for the 'Ladies Home Journal.'"

"It might. You see—you would—in a sense —I mean—you mean—" Why could n't he get it out? It was the best chance he ever would get to ask that one question, he knew. "You see —I mean—you would belong—to me—"

"Mr. Goss, I am very sorry to interrupt you. I hope you will pardon me, Miss Myers." It was the voice of the supervisor. "I have just had a telephone message which will take me back to Illahee instead of going over across the river. The state forester has wired me to meet him there. I will have to leave the first thing in the morning, so I should like to go over some matters with you this evening. You will pardon me, Miss Myers?"

"Certainly. We were only watching the sunset."

"Goss, I want you to go over to Gates' district tomorrow, so I think perhaps we might all go down the trail tomorrow together."

"Certainly, sir."

That would give him her company to the cabin, at any rate. But little chance would there be for any personal conversation in the presence of Mr. and Mrs. Gates, *and* the supervisor. So the three walked to the ranger's house together,—a somewhat startled young woman, a disappointed young man, and an oblivious supervisor whose mind was solely on his work.

CHAPTER XVIII

ON THE PEAK

SUNDAYS in the forest were just like any other days, Jane Myers meditated, as she sat on her doorstep and looked out over the dancing waters of the creek. Her dinner was safely stowed away in the fireless cooker, so she had time for meditation even if she was to have some one for dinner. When she was cooking for some one else, the cooker was released from its ignominious standing of a window seat and put to its proper use, but when she was alone Jane found its very appearance desolating. For lack of human society she had to have the pleasant crackle of the wood in the stove, the glimmer of light under the kettle. It seemed more homelike.

She had been dreaming of the old home that morning, as memory carried her back to the home town in Connecticut and she heard again the faint echo of the church bells. She could hear again the plaintive notes of the small organ and the shrill soprano of Miss Maria in the choir. And then the face of the old minister, grave and gentle, and fine, came back to her. She remembered the pleasant light in his face the day she had told him, who had known her all her life, that she wanted him to say the solemn words that would make her Ned Brent's wife. "But I wonder how solemn they would seem now if I *had* married him," she murmured. She shivered a little as she remembered his grave face during that long horrible wait for the bridegroom who never came and his tenderness to her in the days that followed. And her mind drifted on to her year at college and again she heard the sweet-toned chimes ringing out over the lake and valley the old church hymns which she had known from cradlehood.

Now it was all so different. Was she really the same Jane Myers? Could this really be she, this brown-faced girl living alone in the forest with only the companionship of a sharp-tongued old woman and these two men who had been such good friends of hers? Her glance fell on the cougar skin which adorned her floor and she

[300]

remembered, again with a little shiver, that fearful yell on the cabin roof, the endlessly long weeks of winter,—and *his* face as he had entered the door that morning when they had rescued her. Did he care for that other girl—the one who had turned him down? "That is, I think she turned him down"—Jane always found it necessary to be explicit with herself on that point. Did he—

"*He-e-e-igh ho-o-o-o!*"

She roused herself at the familiar sound, and rose as Bob came lightly up the trail. Burnham dropped from his horse and Bob began to look for grass.

"All 's well?" he asked.

"All 's well," she responded smilingly.

The weeks of springtime in the open air, grubbing up the trail and chopping the lighter firewood had brought back the color and freshness lost during those imprisoned weeks of winter.

"Dinner 's almost ready," she added as she stepped into the house. The beauty of a fireless cooker was that, with known weight, a dinner can be ready on a given moment. Jane began to dish the meal, while Burnham took her place on the doorstep for a moment.

"It's too beautiful to come in the house, even for a meal," he remarked as he seated himself at the table in answer to her call.

"If it stays warm," she answered, "I am going to try eating out of doors."

"Ugh! Bugs, flies, ants, cold meals, sun in your face—"

"Yet you like camping out!"

"Yes, indeed. I love the wildness, the open-airness of it,—when I am out of doors. But here—that's another thing."

"Did you see my rustic table? I made it from some of the planks left from the flooring."

"It wobbles! I'm sure it wobbles."

"My *beautiful* table! And I worked so hard over it! Mr. Goss said it was a good piece of work."

Burnham gave her a quick glance.

"It's fine. And so's the chair. Where did you get that idea?"

"Mr. Goss suggested it. He cut the young alders for it last month and showed me how to bend them."

Burnham inspected the chair gravely. "I think I can show you how to improve upon that design," he said. "If you bend the arch less and make it more solid in the back, it will be more comfortable."

But even carpenter work by Jane was at that moment of less interest to him than the well-cooked dinner which Jane had set before him. The lighter china used by her was always a relief to him. Tin cups in the forests and tin plates as well were all right, but the ironstone china which he endured elsewhere always grated upon him. It was a fastidious trait he had retained from civilization. Yet even in his own cabin the chinaware was the hideous ironstone, "Because, you know," he remarked to Goss one day, railing upon heavy chinaware, "we'd smash the other kind all to flinders in no time."

"Let's go up to the Peak this afternoon and watch the sunset," he suggested, as dinner progressed. Jane left the table to replenish the hot biscuit. "It's a glorious day outside, and the sunset is—well, it's a miracle. When Goss and I are in the mood for it we have been known to

[303]

travel fifteen miles in all to see the sun set over the Peak."

"Where is he?"

"Up in the forests somewhere. I don't know just where."

"Do you think he might come while we are away?"

Burnham turned and gave his hostess a searching look. Jane was bending over a pan of hot biscuit just drawn from the oven and if there was more color in her face, the heat was a ready excuse for it.

"We can leave a note for him—he can follow if he wants to; or wait for us if it's too late."

"All right. I should like to go. But we'll have to borrow the Widdy's pony."

"I'll manage that."

Dinner once over, Burnham hurried off to ask the Widdy for her pony. He was in a hurry to get started, as he frankly admitted to himself, because he was afraid Goss would appear. "And he sees quite enough of her," he muttered. Ever since the rescue in the winter, Burnham had realized that this particular cabin had grown to have an almost irresistible fascination for him, and he had not hesitated to take the advantage which his frequent trips up and down the trail necessitated to become a frequent caller. Goss's time was not at his own disposal and he was there much less often, yet Burnham had noticed that he was there as often as possible. If both of them took their meals with the Widdy it was chiefly to help her and a generous wish not to be an expense to the younger homesteader, but the meal once eaten, the Widdy saw them no more. Jane had invited her to join them on some of their jaunts, but journeying through the woods for pleasure when she lived in them and experienced their hardships was not the Widdy's idea of fun.

"It's six miles up to the Peak by the long trail, and two back by the short one," said Burnham as he reappeared with Dempsey, then added abruptly as he saw the wave of a dish towel, "Good gracious. You're not going to wash those dishes now, are you?"

"It isn't good housekeeping to leave them."

"Haven't you enough for supper?"

"Oh, yes."

"And for breakfast?"

"Yes."

"Then why wash them?" Burnham's logic was still essentially masculine.

Jane laughed. "All right. I don't have good company for a climb up the mountain every day. We'll let the dishes go."

Burnham brought Dempsey around to a block of wood which could serve as a mounting block. "Now—"

"Oh, wait. We didn't write any note for Mr. Goss."

"Oh, yes. You write one." But he looked in the other direction.

"There. Will you stick that on the door?"

"Gone to see the sunset on the Peak. Follow if you can," it read.

He gritted his teeth and fastened up the note.

"Now," he said again, and this time they started off, down the trail. With the sure-footed mountain horses, Jane had only to let Dempsey follow Burnham's horse and give herself up to enjoyment.

Through the cool greenness of the forest, amid the cathedral arches of the great trees, spruce and fir and cedar, they traveled a while in silence.

The only sounds were the ripple of the creek and then the voice of the falls, clear and deep and musical, the light murmuring of the tree tops in the light breeze, the breathing of the horses and the splash of water as they left the springy soil, carpeted with dry needles, and waded through the streams. Now and again they forded a stream whose swift current forced the ponies to brace themselves against it—not the happy, rippling creeks wandering through grassy New England meadows, but streams which were wild, picturesque, romantic, powerful, like all of nature's work in the great Northwest. From the chill of the forest, as they climbed upwards, grassy meadows, sprinkled with wild flowers, broke the density of the forest. The song of the birds rippled musically over the gemlike parks. Here and there snowy patches still lingered, bordered by trickling streams of water, pierced with the smooth, dark leaves and the waxen flowers of the Alpine lilies.

At last they left the regular trail and climbed straight upward, Burnham leading with a sureness of footing which betokened perfect ac-

quaintance with the spot, far though it was
from the beaten trail of mankind.

"This hill," he remarked, as they climbed
through the last bit of snow lying in a hollow,
"I call Paradise Point, because of the flowers
and the view."

The ground up that last steep slope, open to
the south and sheltered from the wind, was
carpeted with wild flowers, of all colors—red,
blue, yellow, and white, mountain anemones,
wild columbine, Canadian dogwood,—a tiny
flower a few inches high, with the dogwood
blossom,—spring beauties, mountain buttercups,
Alpine lilies, squaw-grass, and many another
radiant blossom.

Jane with head bent to the ground, exclaim-
ing over the fragrance and beauty of the sunlit
hill, let the pony climb at his own will.
Dempsey at last heaved a great sigh and stood
still. Jane looked up. Without knowing it,
she had climbed to the crest of a hill overlook-
ing the valley of the Illahee.

Below her,—three thousand feet below,—
raged the untamed, ice-cold waters of the Illahee, bordered to its edge with the great forests

which covered the slopes. The great firs of the forest were no larger than arrows; the river merely a silvery thread between masses of blackish-green. To the north and the south were rounded green slopes, wooded to their very tops. But directly opposite her, towering over all, its dazzling white crown gleaming against the deep blue of the sky, rose the great snow-capped Peak.

Burnham glanced at her silently and turned away at the awed rapture on the girl's face. The deep breathing of the horses, the light murmur of the breeze, were the only sounds. Then at last he helped her down off her horse, unsaddled the panting animals, and dropped the saddle blanket on the ground for a seat.

"I thought I knew the beauty of these mountains," Jane said, turning to him as the afternoon wore away with only light comment occasionally on either side, "but I never imagined anything like this."

Gradually the shadows lengthened as the sunset lights began to creep over the Peak, and the long purple shadows nestled into the silent corners of the lower slopes. Still the man could not find the words to say what he had meant to say. The silence between them was unbroken by any sound except that long, solemn roll, like a far-away organ, of the wind in the tree tops below them. The quiet of the place, the wondrous beauty and solemn splendor of the peak in its marvelous coloring, banished the last thought of strangeness between them. They two, and they only, lived in that wonderful evening. Burnham had seen it before. Indeed, as he had told Jane, he and Goss had ridden miles to see the sunset on the Peak, but it was never twice the same. And this evening it was all the more sublime in its hues because she was there. It had silenced her just as it always silenced him—just as it silenced him now when he wanted so much to ask her that one question. The apparent trivialities of human life were overawed.

Still the lights grew softer on the peaks,—the rosy tints illuminating the valleys open to the light, the purple shadows darkening in the forested slopes below.

Far to the westward the setting sun painted a golden pathway through the Straits of San

Juan de Fuca, softening in the fading light the long black guns that look toward the Far East and dimming the bold outlines of the square-built barracks. Lights from large cities sprang up along the eastern edge of the great inland sea as the mountain range of the Olympics faded into soft gray-blue against a pale, golden sky. In the Straits and on the Sound gray-tipped gulls wheeled and screamed above the ships of ocean, but on the Peak there was only the grandeur of the mountain and the wondrous silence.

" I have dreamed of halls enchanted,"

quoted Burnham softly.

"Halls with tapestries resplendent
And high dreams of painting poets
Wrought for kings and sons of kings;
And I 've gazed when sunset glory
In historic mountain places
Caught and changed the clouds of autumn
Into gorgeous curtainings . . .

"In the face of a sunset like that, one feels that God cannot be very far away from His children," he added thoughtfully.

It was only as they rose to go that Burnham found courage to speak. And then the words he had planned would not come. He had lost them all.

"Jane," he blundered, as she stood waiting for him to help her mount, "is there any chance for me—in your life?"

"Don't—please don't," she answered quickly.

"I can't help it. To-morrow we shall be twenty miles apart again—and I must know— because—because—I love you so."

The girl was silent. Far below the purple shadows were deepening. The rosy haze was softening.

"Don't say no," he begged. "Don't say no! At least give me a chance. Could n't you learn to care?"

Her answer when it came was slow. She had known this would come, some day, but—

"I truly do not know—myself," she said at last. "I don't dare say no. I can't say yes— because—"

"Because—?"

"Because—I don't know."

And with that he had to be satisfied. Of one thing only he assured himself, as he pleaded,— that he stood as good a chance as any one else.

But that "any one," as he knew, was Leonard Goss.

They were silent again as the ponies followed the homeward trail in the long northern twilight, yet with both was the vision of a perfect day.

"One thing's certain," thought Burnham as they came out of the deepening shadows of the forest into the slight clearing around the cabin, "nothing can ever take away from me this day's memories."

At the cabin they found Goss. He had read the note, and gauging the time of their return, had started the fire in the cook stove. For reasons of his own he had not followed them. A blaze in the open fireplace welcomed them from the cool chill of the forest. It was a simple thing to do, and, in the hospitality of the forest its omission would have been worthy of reproof, but to-night Burnham was distinctly annoyed with his friend. He felt that Goss was taking liberties. He could just as well have arranged with the Widdy for their supper had he so desired.

But Goss, after a keen glance at both faces,

cooked the supper and played his part with un-diminished cheerfulness.

"I forgot the doughnuts," said Jane, in a pause in the desultory talk. She rose from the table and filled a plate with them.

"Do they have holes in them?" asked Goss gravely, as she passed him the plate.

"Of course," she answered in surprise. A smile came over Burnham's face.

"Oh, yes. I see," said Goss imperturbably as he helped himself.

Burnham declined the doughnuts, and Jane was disappointed.

"I thought you were fond of doughnuts." She did not tell him she had baked these espe-cially for him.

"Usually he is." Goss spoke before he could answer. "Never mind, Jack," he added in a teasing voice, *"I'll* eat the doughnuts. You may eat the holes."

CHAPTER XIX

HOPE DENHAM AGAIN

DENHAM'S RANCH, July 24.

Dearest Jane:

How I wish I had you to advise me. You can see from my dating that I am at Uncle Mart's, and I 've had so many troubles lately I want to talk things over with you. Uncle Mart and Jack are men, and of course they only see a man's point of view. And Aunt Mary is no good at advising. She 's the sort of a woman who is submerged in housekeeping for two.

If you can't make a word of sense out of this letter, don't say anything. I think I 've lost my senses.

The fire came last Monday. You know what a hot, dry summer this has been everywhere. We were afraid of it, and I had plowed around my land to protect it, just a little, though. The prairie sod after the days and weeks of baking sun were as hard and tough as leather. I

[315]

have felt sorry for you sometimes, up in those
endless forests, hemmed in by those dense trees,
while I had the boundless plains before me and
low foothills off to the west. I could see so far,
and the plains are wonderful, but be thankful
you will be spared the horrors of a prairie fire.
Jack and Uncle Mart warned us, because these
fires come so suddenly. The heat had been
awful, no rain for weeks, and there were days
when I'd have given all I possessed for an ice-
cream soda with a stick of macaroni to drink it
through. But there wasn't anything except the
warmish water of the little brook, and that almost dried up. Everything was as dry as tinder. And Toby and I nearly smothered in the
heat, trying to plow even that little fire break.
The cabin was suffocating, and out of doors it
was just as bad, with the yellow leaves on the
cottonwood half dried up.

The fire came from the east, and just at sun-
rise. I thought it meant rain, but it stayed red,
and then suddenly I realized that it was fire.
I stood there fairly frozen, when Jack came
plunging over the plains on his horse yelling,
"Back fire! Back fire!" And suddenly I re-

membered Woodsey. She is n't the pioneering
type, you know,—not a bit resourceful, and she
had n't even plowed a fire break. I ran for
the matches, and Jack dashed away for Woodsey's cabin. I started fire all along the fire
break watching it lest it should cross that narrow furrow, and watched the flames eat back
against the dawn wind while that other fire out
there was racing toward us, and Jack and
Woodsey still out on the plains. When I saw
them coming back, and that it would be a race
between the horses and the fire, I shut my eyes
and nearly screamed—being a woman. The
fire was so close. But they got on to the
burned stretch just as the back fire met it. It
was awful! The two fires seemed to spring at
each other, and rose high in air, and then sank,
while the flames roared by on each side of us,
but we were safe on that black smoking stretch.
Woodsey lost everything. She had n't waked
up to the danger at all, and even when Jack
came, she wanted to try to save something! He
carried her to his horse, jumped bareback on
hers, and they raced for life.

And after the fire, the sun shone as warm and

[317]

bright as ever, and the skies were so blue, but the earth was inky black and desolation itself, just as far as one could see. I saved everything, but I was frightened, and Jack insisted that I should not homestead alone any longer, though the danger now is all past. We were to have been married at Christmas, and he wants me to marry this fall, and to stay with Uncle Mart until I do. I *am* tired of homesteading alone. I think if I had n't fallen in love, I could have gone on with it, but it has lost its novelty. It will go all right double team, though.

Yet I can't quite make up my mind about hurrying up the wedding. Uncle Mart says, yes. Father never did like my homesteading and he says, yes. Mother wants me to come home first, but you know there is n't much money and a good many little folks, yet I want to go, awfully. Tell me what you think. Even if you are not in love, I should take your judgment, I think.

All my friends say, Aunt Mary included, "Well, why did you take up a homestead, anyway?" Because of Mac, my future brother-in-law, of course. Jane, I certainly did have a time of it with that man, from that very first week, when you stood waiting for me at the foot of the stairs in a supposedly empty schoolhouse, and I slid down the bannister. I never should have lost my balance if Mac had n't so suddenly appeared from room 4. But I did—and he caught the full force of my weight. To my dying day, I shall laugh when I think of his ruffled, angry appearance as he picked himself up, dusty as to clothes, and rumpled as to dignity, trying to think of something crushing to say. And he could n't think of it! Poor little man! It was his first experience as principal,—and even school teaching had n't tamed me down *entirely*. Then that other day, two or three months later,—early in the spring,—when I slipped on a banana peel just outside the schoolroom door, as he was expounding beautiful theories. It might as well have been a peal of thunder for the lightning in his eyes. Oh, he had it in for me! I could have forgiven him some of the many snubs, if he had n't gone straight home and told that brand-new wife all his troubles with me. There was only one side of things to *her*, of course—his side. And what a chatterbox she was! Every chance caller was told all about it.

And that next summer when Billy Dixson and I were in bathing at the ocean, having such fun—now how on earth could we know Mac had arrived that morning? Billy dived for a piece of long white driftwood—we had stirred up the Atlantic a bit in our fun—but it was n't driftwood. The yell Mac gave as he felt the jerk trailed off into a helpless gurgle as he went under. If I 'd been drowned the next minute, I should have laughed. I nearly did drown. Billy actually had to rescue me. The minute we were dressed we went around and apologized, but he would n't hear anything. I had planned it all. Lovely man—and now he 's my brother-in-law, or will be, soon.

And then that winter, he objected to my silver gray dress, on a dark winter morning, in a north room! First morning that winter I had not had on a white jabot and cuffs, besides ruching. Just my luck! After three years of persistent injustice, I did answer back. But of course it ended any chance of teaching for me. He never told the facts about it, of course. Simply said I did n't have a good influence over children. That's as easy as to say of a person you don't like yourself that nobody can get along with them. The thing that bothered me though was, that Mrs. Mac felt it incumbent to explain to every one "how it happened" and talked in her usual fashion. I held my tongue, but she stirred up a lot of talk, and when echoes of it drifted back to them, both of them accused me of talking against Mac.

I don't know why I tell you all this, except that I am so stirred up. The future relationship is the one shadow on my happiness with Jack. Do write me a good long letter, and give me some good advice. I wish you were n't up in those endless forests.

And I wish you 'd fall in love with some nice man—but what chance would you have up there! Do write soon.

Lovingly,
HOPE.

Later.

P. S. I suppose, to be perfectly fair, that it was just as well for Mac that I was n't twins.

I 've been thinking of something Grandmother used to say, that when things got all tangled up, the only way out was to love your way out. I believe I 'll try that, because I 'm sure I would be happier myself.

Still Later.

I believe, the more I think of it, that love is the only way out. And I guess it will have to include Mrs. Mac, too.

Here 's a kiss, Janie, dear.

CHAPTER XX

DANGER

WITH the middle of July, small fires were springing up at various points in the reserve. More men were sent up to Ellison's district when word came of a fire, started by lightning, on the Needles. Goss knew that was a particularly difficult point.

"Nuthin' much, I guess," said Ellison as he started out with men and pack horses over the trail. The trail to the Needles had been the first one that Goss had superintended, he had once told Jane, because those Needles were at the most inaccessible point in his whole district. They were needle-pointed, rocky pinnacles, with steep precipitous sides, covered with stunted junipers, which almost crawled over the ground, so low and scrubby were they, and with coniferous trees of moderate size. It was miles from headquarters by the most direct trail that could be built. The worst thing about a fire,

Goss had remarked to his men as they built the trail, was that it went straight across country without regard to such roundabout routes as trails.

The danger from the fire at the Needles lay in the fact that from its craggy spires the burning twigs and hot sparks drifted down in the summer stillness into the forest below. The column of smoke arising now could be seen for miles from the lookout points.

Between the Needles and the nearest sheep ranger lay a lightly forested tract upon which the sheep men had often laid envious eyes. If those trees were once out of the way, the grazing area would be almost doubled. Showers of sparks and ashes were drifting down, there was little chance of being caught, and the herder hastily piled together, in a natural way, a mass of dry brush in the bottom of a small gully, struck a match, and then quickly drove his herd to the other end of his allotted tract. Up and up blazed the fire, catching at the lower branches as it blazed through the scrubby trees, and then flashing to the top. Ellison, fighting his fire on the other side of the Needles found that some new fire had swept past his fire lines. The area of burning forest had doubled.

Still there was little danger if he could surround the burning district. The air was motionless. The heavy night dews always somewhat deadened the blaze. But the summer had been unusually dry, as the spring had been unusually wet. There was some chance, though not much, that the fire might spread still more.

"Any danger, Jim?" asked a young camper from the east, of his guide one night as the reek of the pungent smoke drifted down to him. "We shouldn't want to get caught in a forest fire, you know."

"Ther's allus some danger when ther woods is on fire," answered the guide. "Ther ain't no wind, though. They'll put it out all right."

"You see to it that you get us out of here if there *is* any danger. Understand that?"

"That's right, Frank," exclaimed another of the party. "If there's any danger, we'll pull out. It's back to old Chicago for me if these forests are going to burn."

Despite the guide's assurance, Frank Wyatt was up rather early the next morning. The smoke was a little heavier, he thought. He looked up the cañon and then at the guide, getting water at the stream below.

"Get up, fellows," he shouted, adding as they roused, "we'd better pull out of here, I think. I don't like the looks of things. This fellow's got to hurry up breakfast, too."

He piled brush on the camp fire. The morning was chilly. It caught with a snap and a sparkle.

Wyatt stood by the fire, enjoying the pleasant heat, in the chill, as the guide returned from the stream with the water for the coffee. Suddenly Jim rushed forward and dashed the contents of the pail on the camp fire. It was too late! As the astonished campers followed the gaze of the guide, they saw above them the whole side of the cañon, sloping backward and covered with dry grass, sparkling and flickering. The brush-wood had carried the flame too high.

The blaze was beyond their reach, nor was there any way of throwing water upon it. By the time they could get to the top, the fire would have been there long enough to meet them with a full blaze. Yet the guide was for fighting the fire, and a war of words followed while the fire crept higher and higher up the bank and began to burn around the trees.

"Forest fire nothing! You're here to guide us through this forest—not to fight fires. D'ye understand? Now get us out of here on the doublequick. We can report the fire as we go down."

There was no time to fool with breakfast. The horses, sniffing uneasily, were saddled and the party started down the valley.

Near headquarters they met the deputy supervisor with fifty additional men, hurrying to the Needles. The fire had burned for four days and was getting beyond their control. One might suspect, but it would be hard to prove, that the sheep men were helping it along. And now these sportsmen, so-called, were helping it further. Goss heard their report with a grave face. He knew the spot, and knew it was another almost inaccessible point. Without a moment's delay, he divided his men and ordered part, with fire-fighting packs, to make all speed to the new blaze.

"You are liable for this, you understand.

You have seen the forest fire warnings. Give me your names."

"My father 'll pay for it, all right," answered one. "He's a Chicago banker."

"He can't pay the loss to the forest, unfortunately," said Goss sternly. "See to it that you don't set any more fires on your way out. Jim," he added, as he put away his report book, "go up the Thunder Creek trail and tell the two women homesteaders to go into Illahee. They'll be safer there. Tell them the forests are unusually dry."

The deputy supervisor hurried on to overtake his men and horses.

"Now you foller this trail," said Jim, as they forded Thunder Creek. "I gotter go up here a piece to warn these two wimmen. I'll ketch up with you."

"No, you don't," said Wyatt. "You'll come right along with us and get us out of this forest, or I'll know why."

"How far is it to Illahee?" asked the second one of the party.

"Twenty miles."

"And suppose we get lost?"

"Yer can't if yer foller the trail. You heard my orders."

"If those two women don't know enough to get out of a burning forest, let them stay in."

"I 'll ketch up with yer inside of half an hour," said the guide. "You keep right on going ahead." He started for the Thunder Creek trail.

Wyatt was too quick for him.

"You will, will you?" he said defiantly, shaking with fear at the idea of being lost in a burning forest. "Now you take your choice—*that*," and he drew a revolver, "or guiding us."

Still the guide hesitated. Goss's word was law in the forest. To win his disfavor was to give up his work as guide.

"You 're responsible, since you 've engaged with us, to get us out of this forest. That fellow has nothing to say about it. Now see that you get us out of here."

After all, any man could make that trail in half a day. He could get those brave youths into Illahee and come back in time to warn the homesteaders. There was no wind. The fire would not spread rapidly.

Jim turned toward Illahee. A mile farther down he met a belated fire guard. His horse had loosened his pack. Jim stopped him as they passed.

"Do yer know if them wimmen homesteaders is out?" he asked.

"I met the Widdy down here by the avalanche. Reckon the other one's out, too."

So they had taken warning from the smoke. Jim went ahead with a lighter heart.

"Jove! What a bonfire that would make," said one of the three as they trailed around the avalanche. They all paused a moment to look down at it.

"Shouldn't want to be around when that was afire," said one. Wyatt took his pipe out of his mouth and began cleaning it. As the others turned to go, he tapped it lightly on the edge of a projecting tree trunk.

Jim turned quickly. That youth had set one forest fire that morning.

"Them ashes hot?" he asked sharply.

"Naw!" said Wyatt. "It's been in my pocket for an hour." He winked at the others. The horses resumed their steady pace.

But behind him the thoughtless Chicago youth had left a few red-hot, glowing ashes. Ordinarily they would have died out. But the avalanche was a tinder box. They fell upon dry needles and twigs, thoroughly heated by the hot sun. Within an hour white flames were licking lightly around the dried tree trunks and the interlaced branches. The second fire had been set as unintentionally as the first, and neither he nor his companions knew what they had done. Yet the deliberate action of the sheep men could not have had more serious results.

It was true that the Widdy had gone in. As the smoke filtered down through the trees and hung in light wreaths over Thunder Creek, Jane, going across the bridge to her cabin, found her preparing to go to Illahee again. Dempsey was saddled and ready.

"Oh, is it so dangerous?" she exclaimed.

"Huh. Ther's no danger," answered the Widdy.

"Then why are you going in town?"

"Why do I ever go?"

"I'm afraid to stay here alone—especially

since this fire's started. Do you know where it is?"

The Widdy continued her packing.

"Is there any real danger, Mrs. Patton? It is n't kind of you to treat me so. I *must* know what to do. You 've been in these forests for years. You ought to know." Jane was thoroughly aroused.

"Go er stay as yer please," she snapped. "Thar ain't no danger," she added contemptuously. "Huh. Sally wants me."

Jane remembered that one of the fire guards, out of pure good will, had brought them mail the day before. The Widdy had received a letter.

"If I had a horse I believe I 'd go in with you. But I don't feel like walking twenty miles."

"Wal, yer ain't got no horse."

Then she added more kindly. "Thar ain't no danger."

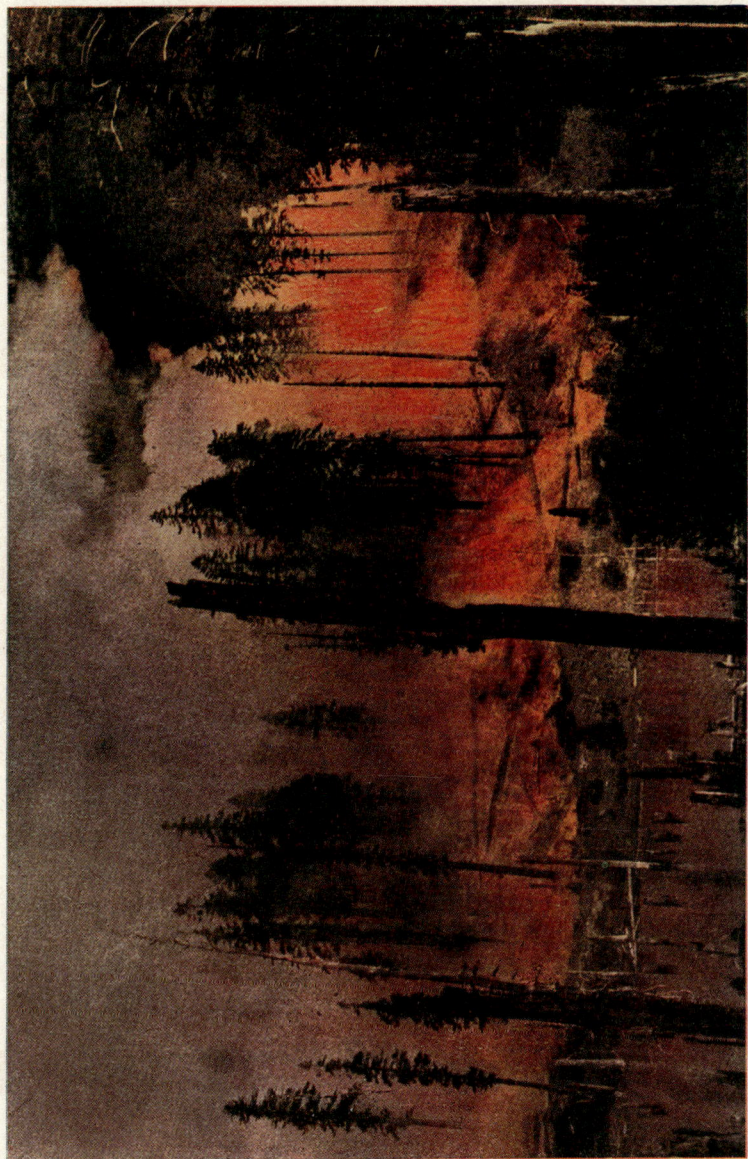

"Whirlwinds of Tempestuous fire"

CHAPTER XXI

WHEN THE FORESTS BURN

THE fire around the Needles was not the only fire in that reserve, even aside from the two accidentally started that morning by campers. Several smaller fires had started from one cause and another, and Goss had just finished supervising the extinguishing of two threatening ones before starting for the Needles. His party divided, to meet the new danger, Goss with the rest of his men and the pack ponies started up the long, difficult trail. The men were of all classes, stragglers in the town, others temporarily out of work, and the hands from the mills which had shut down to fight the fires. The state law authorized their employment. Trained fighters some of them, others were entirely ignorant of the work except as they obeyed orders. The narrow fire trail led zig-zag fashion to the line of ragged rocks from among which rose the heavy clouds of smoke, and up it the patient pack horses toiled, loaded with the usual equipment of blankets, food, dynamite, giant powder, shovels and axes, grub hoes and mattocks, collapsible pails,—the outfit of the forest fire fighters.

On one side the fire had run into an old burn where, five years before, the flames had been checked by a timely rain. The trees were still standing, dry as old bones, as were the fallen trunks with which the ground was strewn. It might burn a week, as Goss well knew, until it burned itself out, and without serious danger to the surrounding forests if they could prevent it from getting further into the standing timber.

Men with shovels and grub hoes and axes were set to work at the edge of the burn, and back fires started from the fire trenches. The sparks which fell outside the trench were vigorously stamped out. In the heat of the August sun, high on the mountain side, with no water available for the fire and none too much for camp needs, the new men began their work. Ellison's men were worn with work and heat and smoke. The reinforcements were none too many. So they fought while burning trees

[334]

crackled and snapped within the fire limit.
They had almost surrounded the fire. Little
real anxiety was felt because it was an old story.
They could win if the wind remained quiet.

But a light breeze one morning carried the
sparks and burning branches across the fire
lines, into the standing timber again. For
weeks upon weeks no rain had fallen in the
mountains and every slope was unusually dry.
Old burns were like tinder boxes. Once into
the green timber again, with the heat of the fire
behind it, the fire leaped and sprang to the tree
tops, and crackled among old dead trunks and
brush on the ground. More help was asked for,
and fifty more men left Illahee for the Needles.

Drawing back his blackened forces, almost
suffocated with the dense smoke which obscured
everything within a few feet of them, beyond
which the red flames leaped and roared, Goss
began a movement to divert the fire. A square
front attack was of no value now. They began
new fire trenches in a V shape, and since the fire
was steadily gaining on them, dynamite was
used more freely. With crash and thunder the
upheaval of the earth formed new fire trenches

while the concussion of the explosion acted upon the flames like a breath on a burning candle wick. Hour after hour and day after day they fought, almost baked by the heat of sun and fire, smothered and blinded by the smoke, burned and blistered by the falling sparks and burning fragments.

Yet other fires were reported, and new men coming to relieve those who had worked for days, had to be sent to the new danger spots. Detailing capable men to take charge of the new fires, Goss turned his own energies to the fire which still defied their every effort. Day by day they fought, yet the fire burned stubbornly though slowly, the sun by day was hidden through the clouds of smoke, the night was lurid with the red light of the flames. Slowly but surely the fire seemed to gain. Yet there was an excellent chance of succeeding if no more new fires started.

Then a new danger presented itself. Toward the east, the direction in which the fire burned most steadily, there was a sudden break in the mountain slope. Some great upheaval had split off the shattered rocks so that for two hundred feet the mountain dropped sheer, with only a stunted cedar or fir here and there, with its roots fastened into the rock. The danger was imminent. From the top of that precipice the flames and burning branches would, without hindrance, blow off into the heavy forest below. Once ablaze there, little could stop the spread of the fire. The crash of dynamite explosions reverberated incessantly as the desperate men tried to throw up a fire break which would prevent the flames from sweeping to the edge of the precipice. Messages were sent to Illahee for more men. Messages indeed from all sections had come over the forest telephones and by word of mouth as well for more men to fight the fires springing up here and there. Loggers, millmen, railroad construction crews, idlers,—every one under the law of the state could, in the emergency, be forced to fight the fires.

Fearing a possible failure to prevent the flames from reaching the edge, Goss with men and more dynamite, fell back a quarter of a mile below, where the bed of a tiny creek, almost dry in the summer heat, formed a natural fire break. Backed by this, new trenches were blown up and new explosions thundered in the face of the approaching fire. But the crash and thunder only mingled diabolically with the roar of the flames, the crackling and snapping of burning branches, the hissing of the volcanoes of sparks.

The breeze grew stronger one day. The flames on the mountain forged steadily ahead, rising at length, in spite of fire lines and the struggles of the men, sheer from the top of the precipice. The sight was magnificent. Leaping and flaming two hundred feet in air, exultant, triumphant, the roaring demon of the hills scattered abroad from its point of vantage a flood of sparks and fire into the tree tops below. Again the men drew back and endeavored to make a fire break. They were almost down to Burnham's cabin now, and the wind had risen still more. Fires sprang up on all sides. The smoke grew thicker and thicker, the air stifling, the men were blackened and scorched and burned, yet doggedly fighting until the breeze became a gale, blowing before it a shower of fire. Sheets of flame, as large as a city lot, left the main fire and sailed like a red blanket hundreds of feet through the air, alighting in fresh patches of timber. From peak to peak, in the mountains of the Northwest, the blaze flashed, and from hill to hill, overleaping at times, the valley below. The flames swept across rivers hundreds of feet wide. The sluggish fires in all the mountains had grown into solid walls of fire two to five miles wide. Far to the westward on Puget Sound, the sun shone red through clouds of smoke from the burning forests, and fog horns of ferry boats and ocean liners sounded constantly as they crept cautiously through the pall of smoke which settled down on the water. Even the water supply of Seattle was saved only by boring inch augur holes in the pipes where they crossed ravines on wooden trestles that the water, bubbling through under pressure, might drench pipe covering and trestle. In every section of the mountains, the fires, fanned by the rising wind, burst beyond all human control. Montana, Idaho, Washington, Oregon,—the whole Northwest seemed to be on fire.

And when the wind rose and the fight was

futile, Goss gave the order: "Save the men and let the timber go."

Up to that moment, he had been perfectly certain that the women homesteaders were out of the forest. As he gave the order there came over him, from somewhere,—he never knew how or whence—the absolute certainty that Jane Myers was in her cabin—and in danger.

With quick orders to Ellison, he sprang on Dick and dashed down the trail. The men rushed for the river. Springing into it, the most of them saved themselves. One group of seven or eight hesitated a moment near the water. A swirl of flame swept down from the trees near them, killing all outright.

Meanwhile, Dennis, with thirty men had started for the new fire which young Wyatt had started so inopportunely. It was the old story, a rough fire trail most of the way and slow progress as compared with the direct movement of the fire. He, as well as Goss, thought not only of the fire, but of the grim results—whole forests swept away, leaving only the bare, desolate mountain side, and the ground covered with

[340]

blackened, burned tree trunks which would remain there for years, for lack of adequate Con-
gressional appropriation, the worst possible
foothold for fire, and a monument to the waste-
fulness of the American people.

Separating his men, with ten below and
twenty at the upper end, the men began their
work. For days they worked and with the fire
well surrounded with an effective fire lane, they
felt secure though their efforts might not relax
for the wind might rise. And the wind did rise.
The light breeze became stronger, then almost
a gale.

It was shortly after luncheon that those on
the upper end of the fire heard below them a
roaring sound. Before they could realize it,
the fire had cut off their trail. "Run, boys!"
shouted Dennis, nor did he need to give the order a second time. Of the men on the lower
end, four were struck by falling trees which
went down like jackstraws in the sudden gale,
and others were suffocated by the smoke before
the fire reached them. Those on the upper end
of the fire had a better chance of escape, yet the
blaze came upon them so suddenly that it was

hardly a moment before they were surrounded by a solid mass of fire. Dennis saw a blur in the flames, a dark spot. It was his only hope. With a shout to the others, he plunged headlong through the wall of fire, staggered a hundred feet and fell in a patch of green brush not yet burned. Others followed, that dark blur the only chance by which they could reach a creek near by. Wetting his coat in the stream, Dennis wrapped it about his head, but the steam later on scalded his neck.

On that exposed point, the wind was blowing a hurricane. Trees three and four feet through snapped off. The shoes of the men were burned off. In the two hours they spent in the water of the creek, shallow as it was, they had to turn constantly to keep from roasting in the fearful heat, breathing through their steaming coats. Tobacco boxes and razors in their pockets softened and broke from the heat.

Still another party, under a deputy ranger, fighting a small blaze when the wind arose, were ordered up to a higher point out of reach of the rapidly advancing fire. By midnight that point had become too dangerous, and in the light

[342]

of the fire, the men scrambled to the crest of the ridge, expecting to pass over it, but only to be confronted there by another fire sweeping up the mountain. Seeing their position hopeless, they started in a wild stampede in the face of the fire for the creek bottom below, through the stifling smoke and heat. Some ran until exhausted and sank without a sound. Others, in the wild race for life, fell over logs and bowlders, and were suffocated or burned. Several succeeded in reaching the creek and made their way to a railroad tunnel. Two blankets they had with them, though many had thrown aside everything. The men took turns in holding the blankets over the mouth of the tunnel, while the others buried their faces in the earth. Yet in spite of the wet blankets the smoke crept in. After five hours of torment in the gas-filled, smoke-filled tunnel, the worst of the fire had swept by, and those who still lived, after burying the dead, trailed their difficult way back to safety.

A few miles from Illahee inexperienced men who were fighting the fires were ordered to leave and go into the town. The fires were threatening. Fire fighting made no impression and the wind was rising. Worn out by three days of ceaseless work and believing they were as safe as at Illahee, many stayed in their camp. An hour later fire swept up the cañon, cutting off all possible escape. Two days later, rescue parties found fourteen bodies, a mile from the camp, together. Nine others lay where they had fallen in the last mad rush for safety. Where the tents had stood lay the body of one old man with his dog. Escape was hopeless. They had died together. And when the rescue party found them, the forest ranger read a simple service at the graves of the dead, while blackened, begrimed fire fighters beside him stood with uncovered heads.

Throughout the Northwest an army of over eight thousand men were fighting the forest fires—fighting fires which defied all resistance, rushing along under a heavy gale. Up and down gulches, across mountains, over deep ravines they rushed leaving only death in their trail. The flames swept through the mountains with the speed of an express train. The defeated fire fighters had no chance to flee for their lives. Of one party of forty-one, only twenty-nine came out alive, and that included men with broken legs and arms, their whole bodies scorched and seared, and many blinded for life. Rescue parties went over trails so rough that when they reached the refugees, the rescuers had to be cared for by the men whom they had come to help.

In the need for men, the government ordered out the national troops, yet they could do but little besides aid in the work of rescue. Even in that, the obstacles were terrific. Smoke like that belched from volcanoes covered an area of a hundred thousand square miles. The trails were gone. Great trees were uprooted by the gale, and the soil was covered deep with ashes. The bridges were gone and the little stations here and there wiped out. The whole face of the country had changed. Great green-clad slopes of forest trees had vanished in bursts of flame and smoke, leaving behind only blackness and desolation.

CHAPTER XXII

FIRE AND WATER

"I WISH I knew what to do!" It was the fortieth time that Jane Myers had said the same thing within forty-eight hours. Day after day the dull pall of smoke had hung over the forests of the Illahee, drifting a little here and there, then settling down under the lofty green crests of the tree trunks. The fire might be sixty or seventy miles away, Jane thought, remembering some statements Goss had made about the smoke drifting long distances. There was no breeze, so there was probably no danger. It might be merely a fire in some slashing, far away over the mountains. The Widdy had said there was no danger. The forester and the mill owner she had not seen for weeks, but that did not disturb her. Even if there were no danger, she knew that both were busy guarding their varied interests against the possibility of fire. Yet again and again she voiced her own fears,—"I *wish* I knew what to do!"

If it had occurred to her to go down the trail to where it joined the main trail up the valley, she might have met the trains of pack horses fording Thunder Creek—pack horses loaded with dynamite, food, spades, blankets, tents, all the needs of the fire fighters farther up the valley. Such a venture never occurred to her. She had no pony, and to attempt to walk the twenty miles to Illahee over a trail she had seen but once, perhaps to walk directly toward the fire—she went over the possibility again and again. Each time she decided against the journey.

Yet day after day as the sun crossed the open stretch of sky over the creek, showing blood red through the smoke, and as occasional showers of fine white ashes sifted down through the openings in the trees, the homesteader wished most heartily that she had gone into town with the Widdy. Her terror of the winter before came back to her. She was afraid to stay, and afraid to go.

It seemed to her that the smoke grew denser

and blacker. It might be that it was the cumulation of days of smoke from some burning slashing. It might be that there was a slight breeze which blew the smoke toward her. Or else it might be that the long irritation of the pungent, stinging smoke had made her eyes unusually tender and her throat sore. She tried hard to reason it out, and to conquer her own growing sense of horror. The nights were to be dreaded. The weird, yellow daylight brought no repose.

But there came a day when the smoke was perceptibly thicker. She felt suffocated; on her chest was a great weight. Her eyes smarted and watered, while her throat was raw. The red ball in the heavens was a duller, darker red, and the yellow light was thicker and blacker. Could it be that the fire was coming nearer? And up in the mountains the men fighting the fire found that the burning twigs set new spots afire, even before they had begun their task of extinguishing those already burning. There were thirty-seven fires in that reserve.

The next morning, Jane cooked her light breakfast at nine o'clock by lamplight. Food was the last thing she cared for, but she knew if fire did come, she would need every ounce of strength. Then she began to consider flight. But where? In what direction was the fire? If worst came to worst, she realized that at the last moment she could slip into the creek, yet it suddenly occurred to her that even that would be a dangerous place if the trees on both sides the creek were afire. She had not thought of that before. The water had seemed so cold and deep. She picked up the pail and went to the creek for water. The darkness was terrifying, but another light sound froze her with horror. It was the murmur of the wind through the tree-tops.

Going back to the house, and opening her trunk with a thought of saving something, perhaps, her eye fell on an old leather shopping bag, with draw-strings at the top. Just the thing! The flexible leather draw-strings would slip over her wrist.

She turned from the trunk and quickly packed a supply of boiled ham, cakes of chocolate, two tins of sardines, and a hard-boiled egg into the bag. With quick motions she slipped into

[349]

her old flannel gymnasium suit, put on her high boots, and went to the doorway. Beyond providing herself with food, the girl had little idea what to do.

The breeze had increased and through the tree tops now there came the deep organ-roll of a strong wind. The ashes were sifting down in a perfect rain. It was broad noon, but dim and gray and somber. A splash of feet in the water of the creek as she stood out on the trail, her bag of food in one hand, the water pail in the other, startled her. Two deer fled past her. A moment later a young fawn, trembling with fear, sprang toward her and rubbed its head against her. Rabbits and squirrels and other wild creatures, even a lumbering bear, crossed and recrossed the trail without fear of man. Jane knew well what that meant. Shaking but determined, she sprang to the creek, laying the bag of food on the bank, and kneeling in the water, poured bucket full after bucket full of the icy water over her head and shoulders. With chattering teeth and full bucket she stepped back on the trail. It was high time for flight. The wind was crashing through the trees above. In the gloom she tried to see some trace of fire. In what direction *should* she flee? The smoke was reddish now, but *where* was the fire? The sudden crack of a revolver sounded close by and her heart stood still.

Down the main trail and up the trail by Thunder Creek, man and horse blinded by smoke and shaking with exhaustion, came Dick and Goss on their last journey to the little cabin. A stumble near the top of the old Douglas fir, a fall,—and Dick made no effort to rise.

"Good-by, old fellow," and Goss drew his revolver. One shot in the head of the faithful animal, and Goss on foot sprang up the trail.

At that moment, Jane, stupefied with horror, saw a red glow in the trees beyond the Widdy's cabin. The fire was upon her. The next, a figure came flying toward her.

"Jane! Run for your life! The pond!" A hoarse whisper from a dried throat. Again Goss had come to her at the supreme moment of her greatest need.

"Wait!" she said imperatively, and picking up the bucket she threw the icy water over his head and shoulders. He said afterwards it was his salvation. Flinging the bucket away, both dashed for the pond, a quarter of a mile away, over Jane's much-prized trail.

It was the broad highway of life to the fleeing couple that day, and though every sense was dulled in the terror of the moment Jane had an indistinct consciousness that that trail was a good piece of work. Not a vine had she left crossing it to trip them now in their mad flight. Deeper and deeper grew the red spot in the forest, and then the flames showed on the other side. Before half the distance was gone, both knew that the forest behind them was ablaze.

Up the trail, five minutes after Goss, staggered a human figure, panting, exhausted, tattered, blackened, and choked. Where he came from, why he came, no one ever knew. Perhaps some memory of a kindness,—some thought of warning her. But the flames were too close and the wind too high. The forest was blazing around him, as the squatter staggered against Dick's outstretched hoof. Too late! With the flames sweeping down on all sides of him, even the creek cut off, the squatter drew his revolver. There was a single shot.

The silent figure never knew when the fire swept over him.

Brighter and brighter grew the light around the forester and Jane as they plunged on, until, with a sudden turn of the trail, they dashed into the water of the little lake just as the fire, crackling and snapping at their heels, swept across the trail behind them. A swirl of flame sprang after them.

Neither had the slightest idea of the depth of the lake, but a hundred feet and more they dashed before checking their speed. Not even yet were they out of danger from the flames. On every side of the pond, with magnificent splendor, rose the sheets of flame hundreds of feet in air. The forest tangle was a furnace. The fierce heat was terrible. Again and again they plunged beneath the surface of the water. From the precipice above burning branches and entire trees, ablaze from end to end, crashed, under the high wind, into the water. The thick, smoky air scintillated with burning twigs and red hot cinders which rained down upon the refugees. On the west side, the high wind drove the flames far out over the tiny lake.

Faint with exertion and with fear, the two carefully felt their way farther and farther into the center of the lake. Goss knew well that some of the small mountain lakes, narrow in width, were immensely deep holes,—hundreds of feet deep sometimes. Cautiously, carefully, holding to each other, they crept on as far as they dared, standing to their necks in water, and breathing the air of a furnace. The water, cold when they entered it, became steadily warmer. Two of the creeks feeding it were actually boiling from the heat of the flames of burning trees and brush along its bank. Fish were not only killed by the heat, but literally cooked.

The hot air, the warm water, the sweep and swirl of the flames, the crash of the falling trees were horrible.

Jane, but for the strong grip of the man beside her, would have slipped under the water. In the fierce glow she could see him now, and had she not known who he was, she would have been thoroughly frightened. With coat half burned off, and shirt half torn off, without a vestige of a collar, blackened and scorched and burned, Goss looked little like a woman's protector.

Crash after crash startled them as the burning trees fell, some into the water, throwing up great waves, others across the creek, others, again, into the forests. The great trees burned as though they were dry match sticks.

It was late afternoon before either of them realized that the inferno around them had lessened slightly in its volume, and that the force of the fire, with diminished fuel, was slackening. There was still danger from the falling trees, crashing down in the high wind, if they crept too near the shore, and the heat was still unbearable, but Goss felt, rather than saw, in the firelight that Jane was ready to fall.

"Shall we try to get in nearer shore?" he asked. "Over there toward the right. The wind is blowing away from us and the trees will fall in the other direction."

The best they dared was to go as near the shore as they could stand the heat and sit down in the shallower water. The swinging of the lunch bag, as she sat down, reminded Jane of her one treasure saved from the flames. It was full of water, of course, but she had taken the precaution, vaguely, to put in food which

[355]

would not be seriously injured by it. It was needed now.

Early dawn had come and the terrific fire had burned nearly eighteen hours, before they dared leave the safety of the water and go ashore at the edge of the forest. But there was no longer any forest. There were only the black, bare, charred stubs of trees, still blazing fitfully whether on the ground or standing. The landscape was as black as though ink had been poured over it, with only the gleams of red to lighten the dull gloom of the smoke. What the blaze itself had not actually burned, the intense heat had utterly destroyed. The trees were still falling.

"I think," said Jane, as she looked about her after that endless night, when a dull light shone through the ruins, and the sun, blood red through the smoke, could be seen, "that we had better try to get out by way of the creek."

"It will be impassable I know. Too many burning trees will be stretched across it."

Yet they walked in the shallow water, turning out every now and then to go around a fallen tree, toward the outlet of the lake. It

[356]

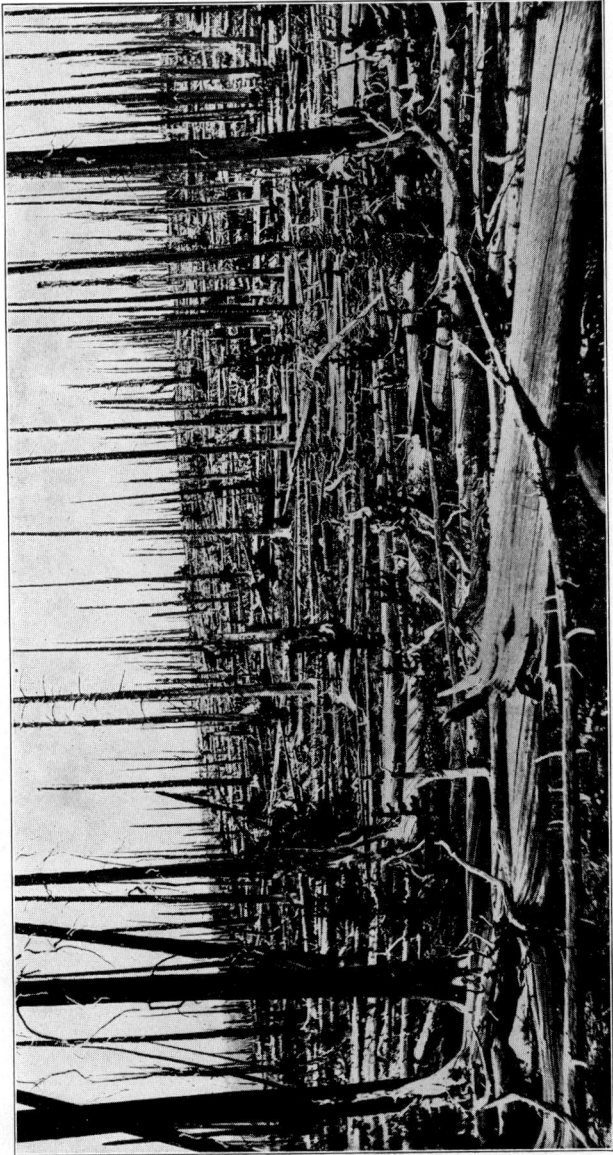

The desolation after a fire

was completely blocked by fallen stubs, still burning.

"What shall we do, Mr. Goss?" For the first time Jane was on the verge of tears. "Shall we start for Illahee? Where shall we go?"

"I am not sure, Jane," he said slowly, "that there is any Illahee to go to. I think everything has gone up in the flames driven by this wind. And the trees are still falling. But we might go down to the site of the cabins. The Service will send out men as soon as possible to pick up refugees—and bury the dead," he added half under his breath. "They would find us more readily there."

The earth was still hot as they began to pick their way cautiously through the burning stubs. A crash before or behind warned them of the risk they ran. Yet it was still more of a risk to remain off the trail of the searching parties.

One whole hour of careful walking it took them to regain the site of the cabins. A few charred stumps, a few burning log ends—that was all that remained of Jane's cabin. On the other side of the creek were a few more charred

stumps and a few more half-burned log ends—
that was all. Jane glanced up the stream for-
merly bordered with trees to the very water's
edge. Charred black stubs stood upright by
the stream; the blackened ground was covered
with other black charred stubs. The desolation
was complete. The streaming sunshine beamed
down from smoky, grayish-blue sky, revealing
grim, dreary stretches of smoking mountain
side, bare and cheerless, with only those gaunt
black stubs of a once beautiful forest.

The shrunken, charred trunk of the great
Douglas fir still smoldered. The sight of it
brought back to Goss the memory of Dick.
The heart-sickening desolation of the place
made it impossible to stay there.

"We had better go down to the main trail,"
he said, hoping Jane would not see the blackened
mass at the end of the fallen fir. Trying to
keep himself between it and her, and to distract
her attention, he asked her for the first time why
she had disregarded his warning and stayed at
the cabin. "Though to be sure," he added, "I
do not know that you would have been any safer
at Illahee than you were here."

The girl glanced up at him quickly, only to
let her eyes follow his as he studied intently
something lying beside the bones of the horse.
A horse's hoof first caught her attention,—then
a blackened human skull.

"Oh!" she exclaimed in a tone of horror, and
Goss hurried her past.

"A horse and rider?" she asked a few minutes later.

"No, the horse was Dick.   He fell at the last
moment and I had to shoot him."   She remembered the faint crack of the revolver.

"And the man?"

"I don't know."

The same chill of fear struck them both.
Could it have been Burnham?   It must have
been some one who came after Goss reached
there.   Who else would risk his life in an attempt to save her?   Goss thought hurriedly.
Burnham had been sent, with his crew, up on
one of the higher mountains.   Could he have
given up the fight, when the wind rose and he
saw the futility of it, and tried to reach Jane?
If not, had he been overtaken up on the mountain side by the flames?   Might he not be lying

there now dead or in need of help? He tried to put his fears away. Burnham was a trained forester, an experienced fire fighter, and a man of good judgment. He must have saved himself. But who was this man?

From the fallen trunks came flashes of fire and long wreaths of blue smoke as the two picked their way amid endless dangers toward the main trail, half a mile below. But the trail had vanished. The blazed trees were down, burned or burning, and of course the underbrush was gone. Fallen trees in every direction blotted out all semblance of direction. Only the crash of the waters of Thunder Creek prevented them from being utterly bewildered and lost.

Goss hesitated as to their next move. There was danger yet of fire. Left to itself, there would have been only smoldering stumps, but the wind kept the trees still ablaze. Fire eating at the roots weakened the trees and even a slight wind would blow them down. He began to be sorry they had left the lake. They were safer there. To leave Thunder Creek and start on that twenty-mile walk toward Illahee was to risk much. To stay where they were was to risk starvation and broken limbs.

"I believe," he said at last, and the crash of a tree emphasized his words, "that we would do better to go straight down to the river and try to follow the shore to Illahee. I am not sure we can do it, but we cannot follow any trail."

The decision was a wise one, even though he did not know that the débris of the avalanche was still a fiery furnace as the tangled mass of trees and stumps, dried by long exposure to sun and air, roared and blazed and crackled, impassable for refugees or for the men of the forestry service.

By the time they reached the river, two miles further, night had fallen, and again they camped on blackened, burned ground, by the side of the water, with the smoldering trees gleaming in the settling darkness. The wind had died down.

The wretchedness of that night Jane never forgot. With the dying out of the gale, came the gray, somber skies, and sudden coolness. In the higher mountains it was below freezing, though only the latter part of August. Light snow flurries deadened slightly the fires on the peaks. Chilled to the bone by damp clothes, irritated by the smoke of ruins which now gave out no heat, they endured the night as best they could. The next morning they ate the last of their food—the two cakes of chocolate. It was forty hours since the fire had come down upon them and they were still twenty miles from Illahee.

At daybreak they began their effort to work their way along the shore. Dodging the falling branches, on the alert for falling trees, part of the time in the water, or again painfully climbing over rocky cliffs far above it, avoiding the charred logs, still smoldering and flickering, lying above the water on the shore, or climbing them, slowly and painfully they made their way down the river. The bridge was burned, they found. They had expected it. Early in the afternoon they reached a point near the avalanche, which rained down upon them a shower of sparks and hot ashes. Blasts of hot air and clouds of thick smoke swept down upon them. The twisted, tangled wreckage of that avalanche burned for days.

On they struggled until Jane broke the silence. "I think I shall have to stop—a while. You go on."

"I shall stay with you. They will find us, I am sure." He spoke as cheerfully as he could, as he realized that hardly more than ten miles had been made in as many hours, and that they were without food.

Again, after a rest, they made another effort. Beyond a projecting point of rock which would carry them into rather deep water, Goss heard a splashing. He wondered if there could be falls there—or rapids. Before going to that depth it would be better to know. He listened again to the steady splashing—and suddenly around the rocks came the men sent out by the Service.

Gates sprang from his horse with an exclamation of surprise. A shout went up as the men recognized Goss.

"Is Burnham safe?" was his first question. The horror of that blackened skull had stayed with him.

"He was yesterday—he's in charge of the water flume at Illahee."

"And the men with me? They went for the river."

"Most have come in—came down the river. Any one else up here that you know of? Or any dead?"

"One dead—I don't know who—at the cabins on Thunder Creek. Did they save the town?"

"All but the outlying houses. One of the mills burned."

Gates had pulled out some provisions while he spoke. Two horses were taken out of the pack train, and a guide detailed to get the refugees to safety. He passed on with his rescue party. There probably were others somewhere up among those blackened tree trunks. It was his work now to rescue the living and bury the dead. They were buried where they fell and often no identification was possible. The work of the flames had been too thorough.

It was full night when they reached Illahee, to find the town still in excitement. The wind had died down but the forests were still burning. Men were wearied of the struggle, and red-lidded, blackened, with scorched beards and singed eyebrows, they tried to board the trains.

Revolvers were brought into play. Men must stay. The town was doomed unless every able-bodied man stayed there to fight the fire.

Alive to the danger, Goss sprang from his horse, alighting on an old broom handle. Without a sound he went down into a heap on the ground. An effort to pick himself up, and down he went again!

"Sprained ankle, I guess," said the guide. "Pick him up, men, and get him on the train. Quick! This woman, too."

There was a clang of bells and whistle as two men helped their guide pick up the forester and ran as rapidly as possible toward the train on a siding. The nearest car was a box car and into it they pushed him. Another helped Jane through the unprotected door, and before she could draw a breath the train was in motion.

In the darkness of the night, the burning trees on the mountains twinkled amidst the smoke like the lights of a city, but toward the west, over the crown of a hill, came the ruddy glow and long streaks of flame as the blaze leaped high among trees.

Day coaches and box cars were crowded with

their human freight. Standing, the refugees were packed tight in the freight cars until, through the smoke and glare and danger, the train reached Tyee. Many preferred to wait there until the fate of Illahee should be settled. The rest, sitting or stretched out on the floor, sped through the darkness, out from the mountains and the forests, over the stretches of sand and sagebrush, toward the city of refuge.

CHAPTER XXIII

ILLAHEE

THE Widdy was thoughtful on that twenty-mile ride to Illahee except as she broke the stillness to ask about the fire. Forest dweller though she was, and accustomed to see the smoke of forest fires, heretofore they had been small fires and easily conquered. But this year the summer had been unusually dry, there were more fires in the slashing than usual, and she had lived in the mountains long enough to know the horrors that were possible if the wind rose.

"Where's the worst blaze?" she asked a fire guard as she rounded the trail above the débris from the avalanche.

"Started over on the Needles—it's burning from there." The Widdy tightened her lips. The Needles were inaccessible except by trails which turned and doubled on themselves so that a man would need to go five miles while a fire went one.

"It must be burnin' somewhere else, too."
The air was thick with pungent, acrid smoke.

"They's eight fires going now—but they's
little fellows. They'll put 'em out easy."

The Widdy reined in her pony and looked
down over the tangle of logs and branches immediately below her. She thought of the girl
in the little cabin by the creek.

"Mother Mary hilp her if *that* gits afire,"
she said.

Sally was sick and Pat was cross, and between
the domestic wrangling and fretful children, the
Widdy had her hands full for a few days. But
the smoke grew thicker and thicker. The children complained because their eyes hurt them
and their throats were sore. Everywhere was
the smell of the burning. The men of the town
looked grave. A ranger with his men went
two miles above the town to protect the water
supply. The brush was chopped away from
every foot of the flumes to the point where it
entered the town. It was reported that the
flames were in the forests west of the town.

By three o'clock one afternoon the pall of
smoke overhanging the little mill town was so

dense that electric lights were turned on.
Many women packed their belongings hastily, in
bundles or in suitcases, and with their children
made for the railroad station. Sally and the
two younger children left that afternoon in a
box car. Men who made for the trains were
met with cocked pistols and ordered back to
fight the fire, and save their homes. The
Widdy and Sam stayed to help Pat. As dusk
fell, the lurid light of the heavens silhouetted
the black houses against the brilliant light.
Until dawn the men worked hurriedly digging
trenches and fire breaks west of the town. Still
there was hope for there was no wind.

Dawn came in cloudy darkness and the rising
sun shone with a ghastly yellow light through
the thick air. The fire was creeping nearer.
The Widdy, like many another woman, under-
took to protect her house. The men must fight
the fire at the edge of town.

As the darkness lightened and the thick smoke
rolled down, the first crest of flame came over
the mountain side. Again there was a rush for
the cars and again the men who fled were met
with cocked revolvers.

The Widdy rushed down the street into the hardware store. A single piece of hose lay on the floor near the door. Picking it up, and noting that the couplings were attached the active old woman started for the door.

"Pay yer whin the fire is out," she shouted over her shoulder, and dashed up the street.

Back up the sawdust paved street, it took the quick-motioned little woman only a moment to attach the hose to her neighbor's faucet and climb the ridge comb of the house, while Sam turned on the water from below. On all sides every available piece of hose was brought into play for the roofs and exposed sides of buildings, while up on the mountain side to the west, magnificent yet horrible, the flames sprang high in air, greedily licking up the tall trees, sending down showers of sparks and burning twigs upon the steaming, scorching buildings of the little town below.

Sickened with the heat, appalled by the progress of the flames whose flaring light shone through the clouds of dense smoke, almost suffocated with the acrid air, the Widdy sat there, as did others, hour after hour, often turning the hose on herself.

By noon every business house had been closed —the mill had shut down days before—so that the men might fight the fire, and at the front, trying to turn back that wall of fire rushing down upon them, stood that line of daring men. Above the roar of the fire the dynamite crashed and thundered as masses of earth were blown up to form a fire wall. And from the fire wall, amid showers of sparks and red hot cinders, crept the first blaze of a back fire. Creeping through the dry brush on the ground, leaping high with crackle and snap as it licked up the green branches, the new fire began its work. Up the mountain sides sprang the flames, climbing up and up, leaping to the tops of trees in the rising gale, until with a fearful roar, springing hundreds upon hundreds of feet into the air, the two fires met—met and leaped and sank. And the women sprayed their roofs and dashed out sparks, while even small children like Sam, with blackened faces, carried buckets of water to the workers. For lack of fuel on that mountain side the fires slackened. For the moment the town was saved, yet still around them the sky was red with flames and still through the streets wafted the heavy suffocating smoke.

The men might yet save the town, unless the wind should rise again. For two days the fate of the town hung in the balance. Every outgoing train carried in freight cars and day coaches the women and children. Goss and Jane came and went. Most of the women were out of the town, though the Widdy, with Sam, remained. And then the wind rose again.

Down the mountain on the eastern side came the rush and roar of fire. Dynamiting, back firing, every effort made by the blackened, exhausted, heroic men, faded into insignificance under the force and fury of that wall of fire. The mills were early ablaze and the terrible heat and burst of flame from the sawn lumber lighted the logs floating in the pond—logs which burned, like ships, to the water's edge. The bridge was in flames. Sparks were falling in showers and half the town ablaze when hope was abandoned.

Men, mad with fear, rushed through the streets shouting that all were ordered out, and lighted by the fierce glare of the fire, every living soul in Illahee rushed for the long train of cars on the railroad siding. The shrieking of train whistles and the hoarse clanging of train bells mingled with the booming of falling trees, the roar of the fire in the forest, the crackling of the burning buildings were about them as the men rushed for their one hope of safety. Open box cars were packed with men and women. Day coaches were crowded to suffocation in the hot, choking air. The smoke was so thick the Widdy could not see a car length ahead of her as strong men fairly threw her and Sam into the nearest box car. The train bells rang again, the whistles shrieked and screamed again, the long train crowded with its forlorn human freight pulled out, cautiously, carefully through the smoke-laden air, and Illahee was left, tenantless, to the mercy of the flames.

CHAPTER XXIV

WOMAN'S RIGHTS

"MUST you go back so soon, Mr. Goss? Only eight days—and the rains have put the fires out!" Mrs. Fairfax sat on her shady porch and looked up at the tall man standing before her, two or three telegrams in his hand.

"The men are worn out, Mrs. Fairfax. I escaped much of the horror, you know, and I am needed."

"I'd like to know *what* you escaped?"

"The rescue work. Can you imagine what it is? Our men go up into the blackened mountain sides, blocked with fallen trees, to pick up the survivors—other men who are blinded for life, men with broken arms and legs, with bodies seared and scarred, or men crazed by their own terror. And they bury, too, wherever they find them, the charred masses and blackened bones of what were once men. I escaped all that, you see, thanks to my fall."

"Don't tell me any more. It's all too horrible."

"I won't. But I must go back to-night and Jeanie and I want to be married—"

"It's impossible!" protested Mrs. Fairfax. "It's—"

"But you see," persisted Goss, with his gentlest manner, "it is wiser and that obviates the impossibility of it."

"Why wiser?"

"Because I can't go back and keep my mind on my work, as I must do, unless everything is all settled. If she is married, she will stay here with you until I can send for her. I don't want her to go with me now, you understand. That *is* impossible. I may not be able to return here for months to come, and I want to have the right to send for her when it is possible for her to join me. Otherwise, I don't know what independent notion she may take into her head—eh, Jeanie? And a long engagement— I don't want that."

Jane sat in silence, smiling a little at a certain

recollection brought back by the strong, quiet way in which Goss looked down upon Mrs. Fairfax. She knew well what the result of the discussion would be!"

"Her clothes!"

"She can buy those after I am gone."

"But to be married without any engagement!"

"That is true. And I will have to admit," Goss said with a glimmer of mischief lurking about the corners of his mouth, "that I have never properly proposed to her. You see, Mrs. Fairfax, I couldn't. I came up the trail to her cabin one day with my heart in my mouth,"—his face grew graver for a moment—"but when I met her,"—and now there was unmistakable teasing in his tone, "she threw cold water all over me. Of course then I simply sputtered. And a little later she kept me for so long in hot water—"

"*Mr. Goss!* How can you joke about such an awful tragedy?" Mrs. Fairfax was shocked. Her mind went back to the day, just a week before, when this same man, blackened and burned, in tattered clothing, exhausted from

[376]

the strain of fire fighting and exposure, had accepted the shelter of her home.

"I beg your pardon. But I have to go right back into it all. My life work is in the forests and again and again I shall have to fight the fire devils as I have this summer—until Congress gives us adequate appropriations to protect the forests. So I'm bound to look at the lighter side of it when I can, just to save myself. If I see only the tragedies—there are too many of them!"

He turned to Jane, still placidly rocking in her corner.

"I am going down to get the license and send some telegrams, Jeanie. I shall have to leave on that nine o'clock train, you know." His strong fingers twisted the telegrams. Jane smiled up at him, her answer in the violet eyes.

"He doesn't consider you at all, Jane," expostulated Mrs. Fairfax after he had left the house. "I can't understand it."

"He isn't considering anything *except* me," answered Jane quietly, smiling softly to herself. "He took me by surprise at first, but I believe he is right."

"And you're the girl who could 'never, *never* stand it to have a man dictate to you,'" quoted Mrs. Fairfax.

Jane laughed outright.

"I tried to argue, but every reason I might have thought of vanished and left me absolutely blank. The only one I could think of was '*because.*'"

"And men do not seem to consider '*because*' a logical reason," said Mrs. Fairfax thoughtfully. "I wonder why? But, Jane," she added a moment later, "not even to be engaged a proper length of time!"

"Yes, Sue, I know. But we have met in such an unusual way and under such unusual circumstances that we know each other as few people do, even after years of married life. True character shows in the forest. And this is all of a piece with our unconventional meeting." She laughed again.

"What is it?" asked her friend.

"The way he stood there and looked down at you a few moments ago reminded me of my first meeting with him, when we quarreled over cutting the Douglas fir. No, not quarreled,

[378]

either. I was angry but he was perfectly serene. He's a man who likes his own way, but he's always reasonable, and what is more, he is always willing to give his reasons. And he has the gentleness of true strength. I'm not afraid to risk my future in his hands."

Sue Fairfax stood there looking at her. "And Bert and I thought you believed in woman's rights," she said with a little gasp of surprise.

"Poor abused phrase," laughed Jane. "What are women's rights? Merely political rights, or the right to be loved and sheltered and the right to try to work out the ideal home? We don't limit *men's* rights to politics purely."

Five minutes later Sue Fairfax stood at the telephone giving orders for potted plants, palms, ice cream, and other things deemed essential for even an impromptu wedding. And when Goss returned at four o'clock, he waved a piece of legal-looking paper at Jane.

"It will mean so much to me to know it is all settled, Jeanie dear," he said, as he took her into his arms. "To go away knowing that you belong to me. And now I will be quite proper and conventional,—Miss Myers, will you *please* be my wife?" The answer was a mischievous laugh and a kiss.

Half an hour before he left for the train, as they sat chatting with two or three hastily invited friends a messenger rang the bell. "Telegram for Mr. Goss," he said.

Goss opened the yellow envelope quickly and gravely, passing it with a laugh to his wife. It read:

"Mr. Leonard Goss,
    Care of Mr. Albert Fairfax,
      Spokane, Washington.

    Congratulations and best wishes. You have the doughnut. I have the hole.

                Burnham."

THE END.